BK 784.54   073P
POLITICS OF ROCK MUSIC
                              /ORMAN, JOH
     C1984   23.95 FV

3000 648001 30012
St. Louis Community College

Y0-BDX-424

WITHDRAWN

 St. Louis Community
College

Library

5801 Wilson Avenue
St. Louis, Missouri 63110

The
Politics
of
Rock Music

The
Politics of
Rock Music

John Orman

Nelson-Hall nh Chicago

Library of Congress Cataloging in Publication Data

Orman, John M.
   The politics of rock music.

   Bibliography: p.
   Includes index.
   1. Rock music—United States—History and criticism.
2. Music and state—United States.   3. United States—
Popular culture.   I. Title.
ML3534.075   1984   784.5'4'00973   84-4846
ISBN 0-8304-1025-2

Copyright © 1984 by John M. Orman

All rights reserved. No part of this book may be reproduced in any form without permission in writing from the publisher, except by a reviewer who wishes to quote brief passages in connection with a review written for broadcast or for inclusion in a magazine or newspaper. For information address Nelson-Hall Inc., Publishers, 111 North Canal Street, Chicago, Illinois 60606.

Manufactured in the United States of America

10   9   8   7   6   5   4   3   2   1

The paper in this book is pH neutral (acid-free).

*Dedicated to the memory of
John Lennon and
Charles C. Colyer III*

Contents

Preface

THIS BOOK ATTEMPTS TO SURVEY some of the implications that rock music has for the political system. Rock has been an important entertainment force in U.S. popular culture since 1955. Now, in the 1980s, it has become the most influential entertainment medium. From 1955 to the present rock music has interacted with the political system. Rock has been influenced by the politics in America and some rock has influenced American political life, as this book will detail. There have been numerous political struggles between the rock artists and the political elite. These struggles have consequences for rock as art and as politics.

Some political scientists in the past have studied the relationship between the political novel and the political system, or between art and politics; but few, if any, have studied in a serious fashion the politics of rock music. This study will try to fill that void. The book surveys elite responses to rock music from the 1950s to the James Buckley criticisms of the 1970s to the punk rock critics of the 1980s. One section evaluates the various theoretical approaches to the relationship between

rock and society as expounded by Charles Reich, R. Serge Denisoff, Ralph Gleason, and others. One chapter discusses rock
music as a political socializing agent and analyzes the themes
of political rock. The power of the political rock song to change
attitudes and to influence behavior will be assessed. Other
chapters look at the relationship between rock music and the
antiwar movement of the 1960s and early 1970s, rock and sexism, racism, capitalism, and presidential elections. Of course,
there are sections on rock-music politicos like John Lennon, Bob
Dylan, Mick Jagger, and Crosby, Stills, Nash, and Young, to
name a few. Finally, the politics of punk rock/new wave will be
explored.

In this type of enterprise there is a danger that one will ig-
nore rock music as music and overintellectualize the perceived
relationships between rock and society. One can be too serious
about the lyrics and miss the true purpose of rock music—fun.
A writer can focus too much on lyrics at the expense of ignoring
rock instruments, voice, performance, production, and sound.
Yet these are common problems for anyone who tries to write
about rock.

In terms of this project, what is meant by political? Being
political here means that one group (certain political elites)
feels threatened by perceived implications of rock music for
society. Being political in this book also means that certain rock
artists take stands on issues in their songs in an attempt to (1)
recruit people for a specific social movement, (2) support a certain world view, and/or (3) fulfill an expressive function. In
short, if an artist attempts to propagandize in his songs, then
the artist is considered to be acting in a political fashion.

The concept of rock music is at times even more difficult to
define than politics. To define it is to limit its possibilities. A
definition of rock music often says more about the values of the
person who is doing the defining than about the actual concept.
Rock music in this book will include various elements of rock
and roll, soul, blues, rhythm and blues, country, pop, folk, folk
rock, jazz, and reggae. No definition of rock will be advanced in
order not to limit the investigation.

Rock music will be viewed as an art form in this book. More
important, it will also be seen as a mass medium for the communication of ideas, values, feelings, and issue positions within

our popular culture. Sometimes rock acts as a force to maintain the status quo by diverting people from serious political thought. When citizens are constantly bombarded by an entertainment medium, the deficiencies of the political regime can be forgotten. But at other times, rock can act as a destabilizing force against the political system by raising serious questions about the values, goals, and methods of that system's political leaders. Viewed in this manner, rock music becomes a possible political socializing agent of considerable importance. This study will try to evaluate the impact of rock on political attitudes.

This book developed over the years as a synthesis of my interests as a rock critic and professional political scientist. In 1973 I taught a course at Ball State University called "Now Politics" in which I offered a section on the politics of rock music. In 1975, at Indiana University, I offered a course called "The Politics of Rock Music," which explored many of the themes found in this book. More recently I have been teaching a course at Fairfield University called "The Politics of Popular Culture," which investigates the influences movies, television, novels, cartoons, sports, and rock have on the political system and how the political system in turn influences popular culture.

I would like to thank the following people for encouraging this project by their words and deeds: the late John Lennon; friends Paul Hagner, Peg Berube, Chuck Colyer, Fred Hannett, Tony and Diane; and inspirational performers like Bob Dylan, Neil Young, and Jackson Browne. The underground group of rock critics/ political scientists like James "Jim" Miller, Bruce Miroff, Langdon Winner and others have particularly influenced me. I would like to thank those rock critics, especially at *Rolling Stone* magazine, who have provided a great rock library to make the study of rock and politics possible. Then there are my students who helped me understand "their" music: the Clash, the Sex Pistols, etc. Thanks to Louis Laurino, Chris Winans, Sal Porzio, Ed McCardell, Frank Morrocco, Mike DiDonato, Chris Pfirman, and "Ralph." I wish to thank the people at Nelson-Hall, Rick Allison and the "Electric Brunch" gang at WPLR, FM 99 radio in New Haven, Connecticut. Finally, I want to thank the Fairfield University Faculty Research Committee for a research grant to complete this project, and *thank always* Reenie Demkiw.

1/Rock and Destruction: Elite Responses to Rock Music

THE POWER OF MUSIC AS a sociopolitical force has been examined by analysts from Plato and Friedrich Nietzsche to former U.S. Vice President Spiro T. Agnew and former New York Senator James Buckley. Persons in power positions (elites) have often reacted negatively to a perceived threat to their authority by musicians and lyricists. In Plato's *Republic*, Socrates warned Adeimantus about the power of music and its threat to the regime. In Book IV, Socrates argues that the state must guard against innovations in music that are contrary to the established order. Socrates noted: "For they must beware of change to a strange form of music, taking it to be a danger to the whole. For never are the ways of music moved without the greatest political laws being moved, as Damon says, and I am persuaded."[1]

Later Adeimantus responds to Socrates and describes the power of music to subvert the state. Adeimantus said: "[Music] flows gently beneath the surface into dispositions and practices, and from there it emerges bigger in men's contracts with one another; and it's from these contracts, Socrates, that it

1

attacks laws and regimes with much insolence until it finally subverts everything private and public."[2]

Nietzsche, on the other hand, viewed music as the immediate language of the will. In his discussion of the Apollonian and Dionysian spirits, Nietzsche saw that science had destroyed myth and that only Dionysian music could revive it.[3] For Nietzsche, the free spirit of Dionysian music made every single phenomenon comprehensive and significant. He observed, "We now know that whenever a group has been deeply touched by Dionysian emotions, the release from the bonds of individuation results in indifference, or even hostility, towards political instinct."[4]

Good rock music, it seems to me, embodies the Dionysian spirit as portrayed by Nietzsche, and it is anti-Apollonian in nature. Thus, for both Plato and Nietzsche, music had political consequences. For Plato the music acted as a subverter of the political regime, and for Nietzsche, music freed the spirit from political instincts so one was on the level of some cosmic/universal apolitical consciousness.

Rock'n'roll music was born in the 1950s, and it was probably the kind of music that Nietzsche would have been able to understand. The music had an important intrinsic power. It borrowed from rhythm and blues, country, pop, jazz, "hillbilly music," and other forms to create a new sound. With this new sound, the established order had to deal with the commercial success of Elvis Presley, Little Richard, Chuck Berry, Bill Haley, Bo Diddley, Fats Domino, Buddy Holly, the Everly Brothers, Jerry Lee Lewis, and others.

Rock music developed out of a social and political environment known collectively as the "fifties." Dwight D. Eisenhower provided the role of the grandfatherly general as president, and Richard Nixon gave his first deceptive televised talk in 1952 in the "Checkers speech." There were bomb-shelter drills held in most public schools to prepare for a possible nuclear war with the Soviets, and Wisconsin Senator Joseph McCarthy saw Communists everywhere. The Supreme Court abolished the "separate but equal" doctrine and ordered school desegregation. This was hardly the dull decade that many critics labeled the 1950s.

Many scholars have noted the sociological implications of the birth of rock'n'roll in the 1950s and they usually consider such music a form of rebellion against the established order. This analysis misses the point that most of all, the kids were just having a good time. Perhaps some young people were trying to escape their solitary and boring existence in the 1950s, but rock'n'roll was genuinely fun.

In 1951, in Cleveland, disc jockey Alan Freed coined the term "rock and roll" as he played black rhythm-and-blues hits.[5] Rhythm and blues spread because of stars like Lavern Baker, Ray Charles, Ivory Joe Hunter, Bo Diddley, Chuck Berry, and Clyde McPhatter.

In 1954, "covers," white versions of songs previously recorded by blacks, hit the charts. This unfortunate practice became profitable for many record companies who found covers sold better in a racist popular culture than original versions. Bill Haley and the Comets scored the economic gains for "Shake, Rattle and Roll," where the original artist, Ivory Joe Hunter, did not. Pat Boone covered Fats Domino's "Ain't That a Shame" and other black hits. There certainly wasn't anything illegal about the practice, but it raised certain ethical questions about the record industry. For the most part, the practice of covers came to an end when young white Americans started demanding the real thing.

In 1955, older people and some political elites started overreacting to rock music. A congressional subcommittee held hearings on the perceived relationship between juvenile delinquency and rock'n'roll. Disc jockeys broke rock'n'roll records during air time to show their disgust with the musical form. Some protective white parents labeled rhythm and blues as "smut" because they felt such music hinted at sexual encounters. Carl Belz in his *Story of Rock* quoted Peter Potter, master of ceremonies on the Hollywood Juke Box Jury, as saying: "All Rhythm and Blues records are dirty and as bad for kids as dope."[6] The Juvenile Delinquency and Crime Commission of Houston, Texas, banned more than fifty songs in one week.

Elvis Presley had enormous success in 1956, and he changed rock'n'roll music forever. Presley was the first white aritst who successfully synthesized the white and black sounds. He became the new "king," and in 1956 he scored some monster hits for RCA records. His pelvis gyrations set off reactions throughout the country. He appeared on the Ed Sullivan Show and shocked many parents, but somehow most of the kids got the message. In Boston, Roman Catholic leaders urged that rock'n'roll be banned. It was during those early years that the *Encyclopaedia Britannica* yearbook coined its famed description of rock music as "insistent savagery."[7] Academicians such as A. M. Merrio, associate professor of psychiatry at Columbia University, argued, "If we cannot stem the tide of rock and roll with its waves of rhythmic narcosis and of future waves of vicarious craze, we are preparing our downfall in the midst of pandemic funeral dances."[8]

The Soviets viewed rock'n'roll as another example of Western "decadence," but right-wing extremists in the United States viewed the same music as part of a Communist conspiracy to undermine our society. Though some songs were banned in the 1950s, elites could not control the power of rock. Moreover, companies in the industry were making nice profits from this new entertainment medium.

The first payola scandal hit in 1959. Disc jockeys were accused of accepting gifts and money as payment for playing certain records on their stations. The king of the disc jockeys, Alan Freed, was forced out of the business after a congressional investigation charged that Freed had accepted $30,000 from six record firms to play records from the companies. Freed's response was to say, "What they call payola in the disc jockey business, they call lobbying in Washington."[9] Dick Clark came under intense congressional scrutiny, but the American Bandstand host, a hero and an institution for millions of kids, came out of the hearings untouched.[10]. Other DJs were not as lucky. Many were forced to resign for reasons of "conflict of interest," and the rock'n'roll world entered into a new low period. If the political elite could not successfully put down rock music in the eyes of young people, they could investigate the industry in an attempt to scandalize it.

The year 1959 turned out to be an especially bad year for rock music with the payola scandals, poor record sales, Elvis Presley overseas in the army, and a plane crash that took the lives of performers Buddy Holly, Ritchie Valens, and the Big Bopper. It looked like all those predictions by critics about the death of rock'n'roll might indeed come true.

From 1960 to 1963, the lyrics of rock'n'roll were for the most part nonpolitical. There were many songs about death, ugly car crashes, California beaches, and lyrics like "sha-na, doo-doo." Of course, the music per se was not explicitly political. To be sure, there were many classic songs (especially Phil Spector's "Wall of Sound"), and most people were doing some kind of dance like the twist, the mashed potato, the Watusi, or the locomotion. Yet rock music lyrics were in a lull.

During this time many political changes were taking place. The civil rights movement in the South was gaining much media attention. Some liberal white students took their spring breaks in the South to join in freedom rides and bus boycotts with black brothers and sisters in the movement for full black equality. The tactics and pressure Martin Luther King, Jr., and the civil rights movement applied to the national consciousness also influenced a kid from Hibbing, Minnesota, named Robert Zimmerman. When Zimmerman moved to New York and became Bob Dylan, his new kind of political protest song would help change popular culture and the rock music industry and would reflect what was going on politically in the early 1960s.

Bob Dylan, if nothing else, liberated the lyrics of rock music. He was at the forefront of the early 1960s movement when he sang political protest songs. Other important "folkies" included singers like Phil Ochs, Buffy Sainte Marie, Joan Baez, and the group Peter, Paul, and Mary. Yet most of this music was not getting massive air play, and the political elites did not have to respond because they did not feel threatened by the music.

In late 1963, when John F. Kennedy was assassinated, U.S. popular culture and national consciousness reached a low point. For some people, the Beatles brought about a restoration of hope as they forever changed the cultural landscape of America during the "British invasion" of 1964. If Dylan liberated the lyrics of rock music, then the Beatles liberated the music. The Beatles made rock'n'roll fun again. Moreover, the new sounds coming from the Beatles, the Rolling Stones, the Animals, the Dave Clark Five, the Kinks, and numerous other

British groups changed many things in America. Young people started buying record albums, and they wanted to form their own garage bands to entertain their friends. Rock'n'roll had suddenly switched over to a new, more dynamic form called "rock," thanks to the Beatles.

When the Byrds electrified Dylan's songs and when Dylan himself went electric in 1965, a new genre, "folk-rock," was born. Sonny and Cher, along with Barry McGuire, whose "Eve of Destruction" was one of the first Top 40 protest songs, also contributed to folk-rock. The war in Indochina was building up at a rapid rate, and there was much racial discord in the country. Then, in 1967, the great rock music explosion took place during the "summer of love," when America was Sgt. Peppered, Creamed, Jefferson Airplaned, Doored, Hendrixed, and Joplined in rapid fashion. Now the political elites had to take note. The music was changing in a fundamental way. In some ways it was becoming more political and socially conscious. The lyrics were not trying to maintain the status quo. *Hippies, love, peace* and *psychedelics* were the key words of the day for the mass media.

While many young people were making idealistic commitments to Eugene McCarthy and Robert Kennedy in the 1968 presidential primaries in order to end the war in Vietnam, Richard Nixon slipped into the presidency with a "secret plan" to end the war. Though Nixon was the "peace" candidate in 1968, it took him until January 1973 to end our military involvement in the war in Indochina. Nixon and his vice president, Spiro Agnew, had to react to the ever-growing antiwar movement from 1969 to 1972, and this movement was beyond their command.

Agnew started coming down hard in his rhetoric on antiwar protestors, the news media, students, "long hairs," dope smokers, and rock music lyrics. Agnew charged that rock lyrics were "brainwashing" young listeners into taking drugs and that rock music was threatening to destroy our national strength. He argued that the Beatles' song "With a Little Help from My Friends" was about the use of drugs, and he maintained that the Byrds's "Eight Miles High" and Jefferson Airplane's "White Rabbit" made young people turn to drugs.

Rock music was slowly entering into the period rock writer Bob Somma labeled as the "Nixonization of Rock."[11] Paul Kantner of Jefferson Airplane sent Agnew a box of newer records from his band to bring Agnew up to date with what was happening in rock music.[12] The vice president had been two or three years behind in his rock commentary. President Nixon relied on impressions about rock music from his daughters, Tricia and Julie. Nixon said: "I don't understand youth music yet, but Tricia and Julie do. There is a spirit there, there is a lift to it. I almost feel like dancing."[13] His daughters' favorite groups included the Turtles and the Guess Who, so it is doubtful if Nixon ever heard any radical FM radio impressions about the new rock explosion.

President Nixon liked classical symphony music and some rather racist country-and-western songs, for example, "Welfare Cadillac," "Okie from Muskogee," and "The Ballad of Lt. Calley." When Johnny Cash was invited to sing at the White House in April 1970, Nixon requested "Okie" and "Welfare Cadillac" from Cash even though these were not his hits. Cash at first felt, "If that's what the president wants to hear, I'll sing it."[14] Yet to his credit Cash declined to sing the songs at performance time.

Nixon had Agnew continue his attacks on the drug-oriented nature of rock music. Nixon said that the government would not interfere in programming decisions but he implied the opposite by saying, "After all, you [broadcasters] do get your licenses from the federal government."[15] John Broger, of the Armed Forces Office of Information, spoke to some broadcasters and said that GIs were rock'n'roll fans and that the drug songs helped in "spreading the drug evil" among soldiers.[16]

Not only did elites label rock lyrics and rock performers as drug oriented, but they also criticized the music for being obscene. In 1970, Country Joe McDonald of Country Joe and the Fish was fined $500 in Worchester, Massachusetts, as a "lewd, lascivious and wanton person in speech and behavior."[17] McDonald's crime, of course, was that he had led the traditional F-I-S-H cheer that precedes their classic anti-Vietnam war song, "I Feel Like I'm Fixin' to Die Rag," by using the letters F-U-C-K. The same year Janis Joplin was fined $200 in Tampa, Florida, on charges of profanity and obscenity.[18] In some cities, the Jefferson Airplane was required to post a $1,000 to $10,000 cash bond that would be forfeited to the promoter if the Airplane did any "illegal, indecent, obscene, lewd, or immoral exhibition" while they were on stage. In Oklahoma in 1970, the Airplane lost a $1,000 bond when Paul Kantner responded to a policeman, who had tried to end the show before the group's encore, by saying, "That's a bunch of bullshit."[19] Airplane manager Bill Thompson was furious at the forfeiture of the bond and said, "Paul didn't offend anyone at all in that hall. This is all part of the same thing with Nixon and the crackdown on FM radio where they can't play dope songs or songs that are considered obscene. Free speech doesn't exist in this country. Who's to decide what's obscene and what isn't; what's obscene to me may not be to you....What is this obscenity bullshit?"[20]

Thompson thought authorities were trying to ruin specific bands like Jefferson Airplane, Grateful Dead, and Country Joe and the Fish. In 1971, Jim Morrison, the late "Lizard King" and lead singer for the Doors, was convicted of misdemeanors in Florida for indecent exposure and open profanity during his 1969 Miami concert, where Morrison exposed himself to his screaming fans.[21]

The next phase of elite responses to rock music, which came after the dope-lyric and the obscene-lyric phases, was "crackdown on rock festivals." Many state legislatures passed anti-outdoor rock festival legislation that was designed to curb the overnight festival. Too many small-town officials had seen the movie *Woodstock*, and they did not want that to happen to them. Rock festivals got more bad publicity after the Rolling Stones' Altamont concert in 1969. At that concert, a number of Hell's Angels went on the rampage near the stage and violence erupted. Meredith Hunter, a spectator, was knifed to death by those Angels performing their "security" duties. The moment and concert were well preserved in the film *Gimme Shelter*.

In 1970 a rock riot took place in Grant Park, Chicago, at the Sly and the Family Stone concert. Sly had failed to show up at a concert a year before in Chicago, but he was ready to go on stage at this concert when the audience went berserk. Many of the young people in the audience were veterans of street clashes with the

Chicago police at the 1968 Democratic National Convention, and they used the concert as a chance to get even with the Chicago police. Rocks, wine bottles, and chairs were thrown toward the stage as police moved in to quiet the crowd. The police soon became targets for numerous homemade missiles. The final, brutal score of the riot was "3 shot, 165 arrested, 26 civilians and 30 policemen treated for injuries in hospitals."[22]

By now the "peace and love generation" myth that had been largely created by various commentators in the media was all but destroyed. Rock music was getting more bad publicity, and the generation was labeled as one of confrontation and hatred. *Newsweek* magazine started asking "Is rock dead?" and state legislators drafted antifestival bills. Indiana Attorney General Theodore Sendak labeled rock festivals as "drug supermarkets" after the debacle at Bull Island Rock Festival in southwestern Indiana.[23] Claiming organized crime was behind rock festivals, Sendak was instrumental in initiating Indiana's get-tough policy on rock festivals. The new law came down so hard on outdoor gatherings that the state legislature in its zeal to end rock festivals had accidentally outlawed the Indianapolis 500 auto race. Of course, the bill was then reworded to allow the race and other "acceptable" outdoor gatherings.

Perhaps the most famous specifically political rock festival was the one in Washington, D.C., that preceded the May Day demonstrations in the nation's capital in 1971. It was the most overtly political rock festival, and it was advertised as such by the promoters. It was an effort to combine the rock culture and the dope culture with the hard line antiwar political groups. The concert was to serve as a vehicle to relax and recruit May Day demonstrators before their street actions two days later. Of course, movement leaders, such as Rennie Davis and others, used the questionable tactic of advertising that all the big names in rock music would show up at the political festival without having their confirmations. Thus the concertgoers did not get to see James Taylor, Crosby, Stills, Nash, and Young, Arlo Guthrie, Jefferson Airplane, Grateful Dead, and others who had been advertised to gain a large crowd.

Early Sunday morning, May 2, Washington, D.C., Police Chief Jerry Wilson made a bold move that had the approval of

Attorney General John Mitchell and his assistant, William Rehnquist, at the Justice Department, who were handling the May Day activities response for the Nixon administration. Wilson had local police and National Guardsmen surround Algonquin peace city at Potomac Park early in the morning while most of the 70,000 people were sleeping. The crowd listened to the few rock stars who had bothered to show up, such as Linda Ronstadt, Phil Ochs, and the Beach Boys. Wilson ordered all concertgoers to leave the premises by noon or face arrest, and he revoked the festival permit that had been obtained legally.

It was a great tactical move by the Nixon administration and most of the crowd quickly left the festival before noon. About half, who were just there to see the big name rock stars, left D.C. to return to their homes. The other half, the real politicos, slept anywhere they could find a place in Washington, D.C., that Sunday night. These were the people who made the claim "If the government won't stop the war, we will stop the government."

Though the administration's tactical move cut the number of demonstrators in half, it also greatly angered those remaining for the May Day activities. The next day the D.C. police arrested anyone in sight who even looked like they might be against the war in Indochina. The authorities instituted the tactic of massive blanket arrests and detention, throwing away the constitutional rights of citizens, presumably under the orders of Mitchell and Rehnquist. The streets were swept clean in about four hours as more than 8,000 people were arrested for being in Washington, D.C., while a demonstration had been called for. Most of the arrests were later thrown out of court because the police had violated constitutional protections by suspending civil liberties with their massive detention.

The May Day demonstrations probably signaled the end of the massive, organized antiwar movement, and the year 1971 brought to a close an era of political rock music that spanned a period from 1967 to 1971. Rock music on the whole was not very political, but some performers consistently had some political songs on their albums during this period. (These rock political artists will be discussed later on in a section on rock politicos.) Rock music tended to reflect what was going on in society. As the antiwar movement began to lose some of its momentum due to government repression and the movement's inability to change presidential policies, the political messages of some rock songs began to disappear.

THE BUCKLEY REPORT

More elite response to rock music came in the form of a hearing by former Senator James Buckley (Rep., New York) and his staff into "drugola" and the relationship between rock music and the drug epidemic. Buckley started his investigation during the summer of 1973 in response to a column in the *New York Times* by former Nixon aide William Safire. He accused Columbia Records and its parent company CBS of engaging in payola in the form of drugs to disc jockeys and programmers to promote records and acts.[24] Buckley did not get the publicity that he had hoped for since he was conducting his investigation during the Watergate summer of 1973. Buckley's final report to the Senate on November 21, 1973, is a classic indictment of rock music as "dope pusher" and is one of the more articulate criticisms from conservatives.[25]

Buckley maintained that rock music has a tremendous power to help in the formation of new attitudes of young people. In his report, Buckley protested the record industry's lack of concern over the drug-oriented lyrics and drug life styles of rock's top performers. He quoted many people in the record industry to illustrate the point that rock is overrun by the dope culture. Gene Lees, former editor of *Down Beat*, said, "For the sake of profits, many record companies have become, in effect, an unpaid advertising medium for products whose chief supplier is the mafia."[26]

Albert Goldman, *Life* magazine rock critic, claimed after the deaths of Jimi Hendrix and Janis Joplin that "the rock culture has become the drug culture."[27] Buckley even quoted Sly Stone as saying, "This business is amoral. If Hitler put together a combo, all the top executives would catch the next plane to Argentina to sign him up."[28]

Buckley quoted at length from a report on the link between drug lyrics and drug taking in the *Bulletin on Narcotics*, published by the Department of Economic and Social Affairs, United Nations, October/December 1969. The article maintained that there had been corporate irresponsibility in the pursuit of the dollar that allowed executives to overlook the harm that rock music was doing to young listeners by urging them to smoke pot or to pop a pill. The report said, "If somebody says [the Byrds'] 'Eight Miles High' is about smoking pot, but [Byrds leader] Jim McGuinn says it is simply about an airplane ride, that's good enough for Columbia Records. Columbia Records at least has a clear conscience."[29]

The report also detailed how it was fashionable in rock music to be busted for a drug violation, whereas in the 1950s if Elvis Presley had been busted for dope, his career would have been ended. The UN report claimed that the Beatles, the Rolling Stones, and Donovan held an amazing power over young people. The report concluded: "Sooner or later, when an urban child, who lives in the ordinary world, not in the pop world where a drug conviction can be shrugged off, is offered a marijuana cigarette or a dose of LSD, he will remember them not as something his health and hygiene teacher spoke warningly about, but as something Mick Jagger, or John Lennon, or Paul McCartney had used and enjoyed."[30]

Buckley applauded MGM Records president, Mike Curb (now a California politician), for his efforts in 1970 when he dropped eighteen acts that had promoted hard drugs through their music. (Of course Nixon-supporter Curb never dropped Eric Burdon from his roster because that aging psychedelic rock star was still making a few dollars for the company.) Buckley denounced Clive Davis, then head of Columbia Records, because Davis thought Curb's action was a grandstand play.

Buckley observed that many people within the rock industry do not feel there is a causal relationship between dope lyrics and drug use. In a letter to Buckley, Stanley Gortikov, then president of the Recording Industry Association of America, noted, "Music does not create the kind of society in which we live. Music reflects our culture as interpreted by the artists who create the music."[31] Gortikov argued that the drug culture existed before rock music came along, and that if some rock acts extol the use of drugs, they are doing nothing more than reflecting the mood that already existed in the young audience.

Buckley was concerned that since rock had become the most popular form of entertainment according to economic figures and since rock music had special power over young people according to many rock critics, then the industry must show that it understands its special responsibility to American youth. He denounced record company advertising that told listeners to "turn yourself on with a diamond needle" or "music in a main vein on Columbia Records" because it used drug code words to sell a product.

The conclusion of the Buckley report to the U.S. Senate summed up the industry's defenses against Buckley's charges and then gave Buckley's comments. The defenders of the record industry claimed:

1. People do not take drugs solely because they listen to rock music.
2. Drug taking has underlying causes; get rid of those causes and kids will stop taking drugs. Kids are alienated and bored because of great injustices in society. Don't blame rock for society's faults.
3. Rock music reflects society. It is, in Clive Davis's phrase, "a footnote to the events within society."
4. Jazz stars take drugs. Movie stars take drugs. Why single out the rock music world for criticism? Besides, what a star does in private is his or her own affair. The companies have no responsibility to tell rock stars how to live.
5. Stop picking on the record companies. They cannot control the lives of their artists. How is a record executive to know about drug usage by his company's record stars?[32]

Buckley countered this defense by claiming that he was not arguing that rock music was the sole cause of drug taking in U.S. society. He believed that even though there was no sound clinical proof to link drug usage with drug-oriented rock music, this was no reason to discard the notion. He said, "It is hard to believe that the net effect has not been at the very least to lower the threshold of resistance among the more susceptible."[33] If rock music was an art form, as most defenders of rock argued, Buckley wondered why rock did not take the lead as a "culture-former" like other art forms. The fourth defense was invalid to

Buckley since it rests on the presumption that drug usage among rock stars was a private act. Drugs have been openly and publicly used and extolled by rock musicians, Buckley maintained. He observed: "The jazz-drug analogy just does not hold up under examination. Drug taking among jazz stars was a private affair, was not referred to specifically or inferentially in their acts, was always seen and referred to as a source of trouble for jazz stars—they could not play in certain clubs in New York City because the police would not give them a license—and was always referred to as a danger in trade publications. Quite the contrary is true with drugs in rock."[34]

Finally, Buckley did not believe that record executives did not know which stars were using drugs or which stars sang about drugs. Thus his conclusion was that the record industry should clean its own house, lest the federal government be tempted to do the housecleaning for it.

ELITE ACCEPTANCE: ROCK CAMPAIGNS

Though political elites had shown great fear about the power of rock music over young people in terms of its perceived potential to modify behavior, they adapted this so-called power of rock music to their own purposes in the 1970s. Rock music began to play an important part in presidential campaigning. Some campaign managers tried to cultivate the youth vote by using rock as the selling agent. This sale by association often took tragic or comic forms.

Besides being the Watergate election of 1972, the Nixon/McGovern campaign was also the first rock'n'roll presidential election in history. Charles Reich's theories in *Greening of America* about the liberating power of rock music for social change were put to the test in the 1972 election. If anyone followed Hunter S. Thompson's account of the 1972 campaign in *Rolling Stone*, they easily caught some of the rock elements in the presidential campaign. Thompson's coverage, which McGovern campaign strategist Frank Mankiewicz maintained was "the most accurate but least factual book on the campaign,"[35] indicated that the book that most influenced McGovern campaign strategy was Frederick Dutton's *Changing Sources of Power*.[36] Dutton, who later became an advisor to McGovern, was the analyst who tried to put some of the assumptions from Reich's book to the test.

Dutton was an academician struck with "Greening of America" fever. He was writing a political science book in which many of the assumptions had a Reichian flavor, that is, young people are monolithic in their attitudes and behavior. Dutton's main point was that the Twenty-Sixth Amendment, which gave eighteen-year-olds the right to vote in presidential elections, would change politics forever. Dutton emphasized the changing character of the American electorate and that it was moving slightly left of center. He indicated that the 25 million new young voters with their idealistic political values would require a new kind of candidate who could fulfill their needs, desires, and wants.[37] Dutton believed that the young voter was a force that could control elections for years to come. The American political system was "greening," and this would be reflected by the youthful composition of the electorate.

If McGovern had not gotten the message from Reich's *Greening of America*, then he surely got it from Dutton's analysis in *Changing Sources of Power*. The youth of America were holding the decisive electoral power. The candidate who gained the youth vote would become the next president of the United States, it was presumed. The stage was set for the first rock'n'roll presidential election! McGovern would heed Dutton's warning: "It is quite possible that the influence of this younger group will be perceptibly higher somewhat earlier than is suggested by past experience; it could come crashing in as a great political tidal wave despite the widespread discounting of it."[38]

On April 15, 1972, actor-producer Warren Beatty and Ode record executive producer Lou Adler produced the first of a series of gala benefits for George McGovern. New Hollywood personalities Jack Nicholson, Julie Christie, Jon Voight, Sally Kellerman, Peggy Lipton, Rob Reiner, Goldie Hawn, and others served as ushers, along with veterans James Earl Jones, Gene Hackman, Burt Lancaster, and Robert Vaughn. Rockdom's Mama Cass Elliot and Carly Simon also worked as ushers. But the significance of the event was evidenced by the entertainment: James Taylor, Carole King, Quincy Jones, and Barbra Streisand. More than $320,000 was raised at the benefit for

McGovern's bid for the Democratic nomination. At the end of the show, McGovern came on stage and told the 18,000 people that "the Beatles sang two years ago, 'Here comes the sun and its gonna be all right.' We'll be back in California soon, and I think we're going to see the sun again."[39] This was the "new politics" indeed!

The second concert for McGovern was in Cleveland, where Paul Simon and others performed. The third Beatty organized benefit for McGovern was in San Francisco on May 5, 1972. Judy Collins performed along with Merry Clayton and the group Chicago. Chicago, under lead singer Robert Lamm's influence, was becoming more political. Chicago had a drive at each of its concerts to get young people to register to vote. The group's album in 1972 displayed the slogan "Use the Power—Vote." That slogan also appeared on other rock groups' publicity (for example, the Beach Boys).

Rock impressario Bill Graham produced the San Francisco benefit, the first he had done for a politician. Graham said, "I'm not that political. I'm not sure if McGovern's the right man, but he talks straight."[40] Judy Collins was supporting McGovern because of Nixon's outrageous Vietnam policy. Clayton backed McGovern because, she said, "He's a bad mother."[41]

The fifth benefit for McGovern was held in Madison Square Garden for more than 20,000 people. Beatty raised $250,000 for McGovern at this benefit. The theme of the concert was "Together with McGovern," and the show saw the reunions of Simon and Garfunkel, Peter, Paul and Mary, and Nichols and May.[42] Voter registration went on as usual, and even Dionne Warwick sang for McGovern. The celebrity ushers continued to do their jobs, too.

All told, at the end of the benefits, Beatty had persuaded Barbra Streisand, James Taylor, Carly Simon, Joni Mitchell, Carole King, Chicago, Merry Clayton, Paul Simon, Art Garfunkel, Peter, Paul and Mary, Dionne Warwick, Judy Collins, Country Joe McDonald, Three Dog Night, Kris Kristofferson, and many other stars to perform for or support McGovern. The shows probably raised more than $1 million, and the benefits were a much cleaner way to raise political campaign contributions than through corporate gifts and illegal contributions.

With McGovern campaign strategists pushing to register 18 million new voters and expecting 75 percent of those votes, President Nixon and his Committee to Reelect the President staff decided that they were not going to be outdone. The stakes were very high. Nixon decided to enter into the rock bonanza and attempt to register many new young Republicans.

The president and the CREEP staff went "heavy" in 1972. "Heavy" does not necessarily refer to their illegal campaign tactics, but rather to the "Nixon Youth Shows," organized by CREEP and Mike Curb, the antidrug president of the middle-of-the-road record label MGM. Sammy Davis, Jr., who had just broken into the rock market with his rendition of "Candyman" on the MGM label, performed at the "Sammy Davis, Jr., Youth Show" at the Republican National Convention. Mike Curb and the Congregation also did a set at the convention. Other MGM acts were booked in Los Angeles, Chicago, and Washington, D.C., in a series of "Winners Concerts 1972."[43]

Mike Viner, another MGM executive, explained why the president was getting into the youth concert trip, "The president is cognizant for the first time of the youth movement and wants to show that no party [presumably the Democratic party] can assume the youth belongs to them."[44]

As it turned out, the youth vote was split. The results of this historic rock'n'roll campaigning to gain the youth vote of America were tragic. Only 6 million new voters were registered, about one-fourth of Dutton's prediction. Only 55 percent of the total electorate bothered to turn out, and the lowest turnout rate was for people eighteen to twenty-one. Ironically most polls showed that Richard Nixon was perceived as more moral, honest, just, decisive, and trustworthy than George McGovern, whom Robert Kennedy had labeled the "most decent man" in the Senate. McGovern just barely carried the college vote 49 percent to 46 percent, while Nixon won going away in the noncollege youth vote.

America had not greened, and the young people were not monolithic in their political attitudes, values, or behavior. Nixon had not only used illegal campaign tactics to win the 1972 election, but he even carried the eighteen to twenty-four-year-old vote. The latter fact put a damper on the "greening" theories, and perhaps John Lennon had always been correct. The dream was over!

The 1972 election brought on the institutionalization of rock'n'roll campaigning. Recent presidential campaigns reveal how campaign strategists embark on the perpetual search for the youth vote. Most of the benefits are to raise money and, more importantly, to draw the performers' fans into supporting a candidate in the process. This sale by association process reveals much about American politics. In fact, an analysis of a presidential candidate in terms of rock potential and rock culture can reveal something about that candidate's chances for electoral success.

THE 1976 ROCK 'N' ROLL PRESIDENTIAL SWEEPSTAKES

In terms of rock culture, the 1976 presidential election represented the new power that rock music held within presidential politics. Under the 1974 campaign finance laws, individuals are allowed to give only $1,000 to their favorite presidential candidate, but because of a loophole in the act, entertainers are allowed to do benefits and donate their services and the gate to a politician. Rock musicians, promoters, and record label owners were thus in a position to become the fat cats of the 1976 presidential election. They played an especially important role in helping candidate Jimmy Carter.

The rock scorecard for 1976 read as follows:

1. Jimmy Carter had support from Phil Walden and Capricorn Records, from Allman Brothers Band, the Marshall Tucker Band, and an endorsement from Hunter S. Thompson of *Rolling Stone* magazine.
2. Jerry Brown had support from Linda Ronstadt, Jackson Browne, the Eagles, Chicago, Helen Reddy, and others.
3. Morris Udall had Mary Travers and Harry Belefonte.
4. Gerald Ford had his rock celebrity son, Jack Ford, and Sonny Bono.
5. Fred Harris had Arlo Guthrie and Harry Chapin.

Obviously the quality of the rock support varied, and the real battle of the rock groups was between Jimmy Carter's rock money and Jerry Brown's rock money.

Rock groups had the ability to raise more than $100,000 for a candidate in one night's work and to donate this money to the candidate of their choice (usually the candidate that their record executives supported). Then the candidate would apply this money to the provisions for federal matching funds and walk away with double the take. This kind of fast money helped candidate Jimmy Carter keep his early primary drive going and increase his early cash flow at a critical time when he was still trying to be perceived as a winner. Without the rock money, the Carter campaign would have found it difficult to do the things it had to do in Iowa and New Hampshire.

Carter was a candidate who, as governor of Georgia, had once hosted Bob Dylan at the Governor's mansion in 1974. He was a candidate who liked to quote Dylan on the campaign trail. Carter personally knew Greg Allman of the Allman Brothers Band, and he was especially friendly with Phil Walden of Capricorn Records, in Macon, Georgia.

Jerry Brown's connection to the rock industry came from the fact that he had dated Linda Ronstadt, who along with RKO programmer Paul Drew convinced some of the big acts for Electra/Asylum Records to perform for Brown.[45] Both the Carter and the Brown campaigns in 1976 had workers known as "rock coordinators," which shows the importance that rock music dollars played on the primary trail.

It is not clear from the experience of 1976 whether candidates Carter or Brown really liked rock music. Other than "Ballad of a Thin Man," Carter never was specific about which Dylan songs he owned and listened to regularly, and Brown appeared to be just tolerating the Eagles and Jackson Browne. It was clear though that the money raised by rock performers was received with gratitude.

The performers could not influence the candidates' policy stands, and, more important, the performers could not influence the young people who attended their concerts to support a specific candidate. Most of the people who attended the concerts came to hear the music and to see rock superstars; they did not come for the politics. Yet their money was going to a candidate who was running for president of the United States. The Eagles'

Glenn Frey maintained, "People can trust me and the money I raise a lot more than the oil companies."[46] However, the influx of rock money into the political system during the 1976 presidential primaries raised new questions about the ethics of "fat cats" and fast money.

Later, when candidate Carter became President Carter, he remembered the rock industry. Carter invited rock stars like Gregg Allman, Cher Bono, and even John Lennon to his inaugural party. However, Carter liked country and western music more, and he also invited Willie Nelson, Charlie Daniels, Emmylou Harris, and others to perform White House concerts. Moreover, the record company executives got tough antipiracy legislation from the Carter administration.

ELITE RESPONSES TO ROCK MUSIC IN THE 1980s

Political elites continued to try to integrate rock music into their 1980 election campaigns in the form of fundraisers, political commercials, and celebrity testimonials. Yet rock did not have the impact in 1980 that it had in the 1976 campaign. President Carter was no longer perceived to be the candidate who had some support within the rock music industry. California Governor Jerry Brown had most of the good rock music money lined up, but it became irrelevant since Brown was unable to generate any support in his challenge to Carter during the Democratic primaries because of such political circumstances as Massachusetts Senator Edward Kennedy's candidacy, the hostage situation in Iran, and the Soviet invasion of Afghanistan.

Once again, it was shown that there was no correlation between the ability to raise money through rock concerts and the ability to win an election. Rock money was important in keeping the candidacy of independent John Anderson going when Anderson needed some "fast" cash. Rock performers like the Cars and James Taylor did some benefits for Anderson. Although they were able to fulfill the function of raising money, rock performers were unable to influence directly the votes of their fans. Rock music had not turned people on to the political system as some hoped it would.

An end of the so-called rock and roll dream can best be seen in the election of President Ronald Reagan in 1980. Reagan was the candidate who had the lowest rock-culture potential, yet he carried the youth vote in the 1980 presidential election among those few young people who went to the polls. The fears that some social commentators had in the late 1960s that the United States would become a political system, as portrayed in the movie *Wild in the Streets* (where rock stars rule the country and no one over thirty was to be trusted), were forever allayed. However, rock politicos continued to play a part in the political system. Stephen Stills, Carly Simon, James Taylor, and others did benefits for young Democratic congressional challengers in the 1982 elections, such as Toby Moffett of Connecticut. Jackson Browne and others developed a group of entertainers who were decidedly antinuclear. These rock activists used their talents to raise money for their social causes.

2/Student Activism, Rock Music, and Social Change

THE LATE 1960s AND EARLY 1970s have been referred to by many as an "age of protest" among the younger generation. The term "movement" has been used to cover an almost endless stream of political persuasions: the black movement, the civil rights movement, the antiwar movement, the student rights movement, the women's movement, the Chicano movement, the Puerto Rican movement, the gay movement, and the American Indian movement. The political attitudes of various movement people on selected issues usually ranged from liberal to radical, and there was an emphasis by some movement leaders on creating "actions." While this plethora of protest activity by young people is noted by academicians, there is some controversy over the start and the decline of student protest activity in terms of exact years.[1] Most scholars date the beginning of 1960s student activism to 1964 with the Berkeley free speech movement,[2] while the decline of student activism has been reported by various analysts as occurring in 1971, 1972, or 1973.[3]

The scope and intensity of the student protests have been charted by various educational and governmental concerns.[4]

Most researchers agree that the height of student protest activity was reached in May 1970 after the invasion of Cambodia and the killing of four people at Kent State University by National Guard troops.[5] With this increased activity of student protests, burden fell upon political scientists to explain this "new" behavior. At first some political scientists voiced the traditional wisdoms that student protest activity was "deviant,"[6] "counterproductive,"[7] "irrational,"[8] "undemocratic,"[9] and dysfunctional for the political system. But these claims relied upon 1950s and early 1960s political realities, along with a dose of upper- and middle-class chauvinism. For example, Seymour Lipset has written: "A high incidence of intense student political activity is in some sense an indication of the failure of the university as an academic community, particularly since in most cases such activity involves a rejection of the intellectual leadership of the faculty, a denigration of scholarship to a more lowly status than that of politics within the university itself....The greater the pressure placed on the students to work hard in order to retain their position in the university, the less they will participate in politics of any kind."[10] Yet the value-laden labeling offered by some political and social scientists still had not offered any explanations for the origins of student protest activity in the years 1965 to 1971.

As student protest activity became an important force during these times, and also because many of their own students were becoming involved in political activity, some political scientists were forced to reevaluate their views about the dynamics of protest activity within a democratic system. Specialists in political socialization were forced to deal with difficult questions on the origin of student protest. After all, weren't most of the middle- and upper-middle-class, white students who were participating in protest activity the same ones that Easton and Dennis,[11] Greenstein,[12] and Hess and Torney[13] described as idealizing institutions such as government, the president, the U.S. political system, the democratic process, the political party system, and voting? If that is the case, what changed their early socialization? Or were they just the deviants from the Easton, Dennis, Greenstein, and Hess and Torney studies? The stabilizing function of political socialization must have broken down somewhere to allow these 1950s grade-school students to take to the streets in the late 1960s and early 1970s.[14]

There was, during the period 1965 to 1971, a rush to explain. Theories for student protest activity began to multiply. Such explanations often said more about the biases and values of the researcher than about the phenomenon itself. Many explanations served to denigrate and devalue the protests themselves as researchers tried to explain away student unrest.[15] Part of the problem was that many of the analysts often spoke in monolithic terms about young people, for example, "the movement," "the Woodstock generation," and "the youth of America."[16] But the youth of the United States were not all liberal, committed, and antiwar as a monolithic group, as Charles Reich and George McGovern would find out later in the 1972 presidential election. Only some young people participated in these activities; for others it was still "business as usual."[17] The ones who did participate often became involved for various reasons, which made explanation of protest behavior more difficult.

Another problem to which some observers succumbed might be labeled "the Berkeley problem." Often analysts based their observations on a small number of hard-core Berkeley student activists and radicals, and then tried to apply their findings to the whole United States phenomenon of student activism.[18] Others established composites of the quintessential student radical by interviewing small numbers of radicals.[19] Both strategies, which drew from skewed samples, could not explain student protest behavior in the United States; rather, the explanations only approached the unique cases.

Some approaches to student protest activity during the years 1965 to 1971 are:

- Psychoanalytic approach
    Expressive function notion
- Cognitive developmental approach
- Social learning approach
    Civic education perspective
    Imitation view

Revolutionary consciousness
Direct personal political experiences
Rational-activist goal-directed instrumental behavior

PSYCHOANALYTIC APPROACH

The psychoanalytic approach explains protest behavior in terms of deviant behavior; the psychopathological behavior is a result of psychosexual maladjustments during early childhood. The government might represent an authoritarian family structure, or the president might represent an evil father figure. Most protestors then were just expressing their hatred for their parents or sibling when they took to the streets in protest. The seeds were sown in the early childhood (one to five years old) of the protestor. The deviant and the abnormal were all in the streets because of their own deep-rooted, personal, psychosexual problems.

Psychological explanations of student protest behavior can take many forms. In terms of Hess and Torney's models of political socialization, the psychoanalytic approach might be subsumed under "interpersonal transfer model" and "identification model."[20] Unfortunately, Sigmund Freud was only occasionally explicit in detailing the specific aspects of his personality theory as it related to politics.[21] However, this has not stopped other analysts from applying Freudian concepts to explain political protest. For example, Lewis Feuer attempts to relate Freudian theory to the understanding of student politics in his *The Conflict of Generations*.[22] An unsuccessful resolution of the Oedipus complex by males will result in their continued hostility toward their father, and other authority figures may symbolically take the place of the father and thus come in for hostile actions.[23] Under conflict of generations, Feuer includes:

1. hostile parent-child relationships;
2. actual conflict and struggle between parents and children;
3. distant relations between parents and children;
4. rejection of parental values by children;
5. "de-authorization" of the older generation by the younger generation;
6. alienation from the older generation by the younger generation;

7. unresolved Oedipal crises on the part of the younger generation;
8. subjection of the younger generation to harsh child-rearing practices;
9. emotional rebellion on the part of the younger generation against the older generation (which is distinct from more "rational" rebellion of other groups such as workers who rebel against long hours).[24]

As Keniston has noted, the idea that the student activist displaces his or her rebellion of parental authority on the political authority has become a popular hypothesis.[25]

Other applications of psychological approaches to student activism can be grouped under "alienation" and "frustration-aggression" views. Aberbach has noted that alienation is both one of the most popular and one of the vaguest concepts used by contemporary social scientists.[26]

Keniston requires four questions in researching alienation:

1. Focus: Alienated from what?
2. Replacement: What replaces the old relationship? (This might more crisply be referred to as the form of the alienation.)
3. Mode: How is the alienation manifested?
4. Agent: What is the agent (cause) of the alienation?[27]

Using an alienation framework, Keniston has described the process of radicalization, which consists of two changes: "The first is a change in the perceptions of social reality, mediated through personal confrontation with social inequity and leading through disillusion with existing institutions for social reform to the beginnings of a radical reinterpretation of sociopolitical reality. Concurrent with this articulation of a radical outlook, a process of personal activation and engagement occurs."[28]

Robert Lane has noted that an important function served by political participation is the relief of "intrapsychic tensions."[29] When intrapsychic tension does find political expression, it comes about in two ways: (1) the use of political participation as a means of blocking out the tension, distracting the individual from his or her personal troubles, and (2) the use of political participation as a means of rationalizing the resolution of a troublesome impulse through socially acceptable terms.[30]

The "expressive function" notion suggests that participation in protests provides a cathartic release for participators.[31] As Milbrath has noted, "Demonstrations also provide an important expressive outlet for pent-up feelings of resentment and dis-satisfaction."[32] Fulfilling the expressive function is more impor-tant than the consequences of one's action in relationship to a possible instrumental goal. Milbrath wrote: "Participating in a demonstration, shouting a protest, engaging in political argu-ment, pledging allegiance are examples of specific acts that in most situations are expressive. The classification is one of moti-vation and emphasis; such acts may have instrumental conse-quences."[33] Student activists were just expressing themselves and releasing their frustration, according to this view. In a sim-ple version of this approach, the frustration-aggression hypothesis is used to explain protest activity. Yet for the "ex-pressive function" camp, the expression is the important thing, not the blocked goal, the means of the blocking, or the anxieties.

COGNITIVE DEVELOPMENTAL APPROACH

The cognitive developmental approach[34] posits the notion that students who have reached a stage of principled moral reason-ing and reflect a high degree of moral and cognitive development tend to be more active in sociopolitical protests. There is a high degree of association between principled moral reasoning and political protest/social action.[35] Haan, Smith, and Block found, in general, that "students of principled moral reasoning, as con-trasted with the conventionally moral, were more active in political-social matters, particularly in protest; their views on current issues were more discrepant from their parents, who themselves were politically liberal; their self and ideal concep-tualizations emphasized interpersonal reactivity and obligation, self-expressiveness, and a willgness to live in opposition. Percep-tions of parental relationships suggest that little conflict or separation occurred in the families of the conventionally moral with more in those of the principled."[36]

Thus the protestors are acting out of a high sense of moral outrage, which is related to injustices perceived by them. Haan, Smith, and Block used Kohlberg's classification of moral judg-ment into levels and stages of development: level I (premoral—

stage 1: obedience and punishment orientation, and stage 2: instrumental relativists), level II (conventional—stage 3: personal concordance, and stage 4: law and order), and level III (principled—stage 5: social contract, and stage 6: individual principles).[37] While principled students tend to be more active in political protest, young people of conventional moral reasoning are inactive.

The morally conventional person, according to Haan, Smith, and Block, "does not often come to doubt the status quo, unless representatives of that order disappointingly and clearly prove themselves unworthy of their positions."[38] For the premoral instrumental relativists, males tend to be politically radical, active protestors while women are political moderates and inactive.[39] Thus protestors were subsumed under stages 5 and 6 of moral development and under stages 1 and 2 (males only).

SOCIAL LEARNING APPROACH

The social learning approach argues that protest behavior is learned behavior. Thus, one's propensity toward protest behavior is not determined by early psychosexual adjustments from ages one through five, nor is one's possible protest activity explained by a higher level of cognitive and moral development. This seems obvious since people from all levels of moral development and cognitive skills have participated in and refrained from protest activity. Protest behavior may be explained through the interaction of the individual with various environmental stimuli and positive or negative reinforcements.

The social learning approach has many variants. Much of the literature on student protest activity in the 1960s focuses on the family as the important political socializing agent. Flacks found that the activists he studied tended to come from liberal or radical families, whereas nonactivists tended to come from more moderate or conservative families.[40] Keniston has concurred,[41] and Lipset has written that "leftist students are largely the children of leftist or liberal parents."[42] Yet Douglas found that the family was not a leading political socialization agent for his Indonesian student activists,[43] and Krauss's data on Japanese student radicals shows that the family is an indirect, rather than direct, force in socialization of radical beliefs.[44]

Finally, Wood finds evidence to support his middle range theory, which reconciles Flacks's "direct value transmission" and Feuer's "conflict of generations." Wood contends that "many activists act out radical political values that are derived from their parents' radical political values or culturally unconventional values; yet the activists come into conflict with their parents because the activists feel the parents have not lived up to their own political or cultural values."[45]

In the social learning approach the environment is important in terms of interaction with the individual. Student politics are often characterized by a degree of pure ideological concerns; that is, concerns not tainted by partisan politics or personal material gain.[46] Student politics can also be characterized by a naive conception and approach to the problems that confront a society, and students too often seek all-encompassing solutions to key issues that face society. In many nations there is a permissive and respectful attitude toward student political activity in that student actions are viewed as a "sowing of wild oats" period in one's life. Therefore, these actions are not usually subjected to severe government repression that would take place if some other sector of society, such as labor unions, were involved in the action.[47] Obviously, there is a certain breaking point that many student groups push past, and then the once-tolerant government is forced to repress certain activities.

In the university community, the student usually takes part in his or her first "away from family" experience and is united with other students having the same experience. Students feel a need for independence and self-expression, and many times this takes the form of political activity. The concentration of a large number of students at one location facilitates student-movement communications. The presence of large numbers of students with similar interests also facilitates the creation of all kinds of organizational activities, including political groups. Some students can develop a strong sense of community and yet a feeling of alienation from the traditional patterns of society. Despite a great record of student political activity, many scholars have tended to neglect student movements, as Lipset has pointed out: "Marxists, though often the beneficiaries of student protest, have felt that the predominantly bourgeois students could not have played a crucial role in creating, leading, and sustaining "proletarian" movements, and non-Marxists seem to have shared their bias."[48] Many scholars have been baffled by the web of related environmental factors that must be untangled before they can investigate student protest activity. And since student generations last only a few years, student movements and organizations do not leave good records behind them for analysis, according to Lipset.[49]

Another focus in the social learning approach is on the school system as a political socializing agent. This perspective argues that protesting students learned well the American ethic of citizen participation. The "civic education" view argues that protesting students internalized the democratic notions of citizen worth, personal efficacy, citizen duty, and expression of political viewpoint. Students wanted to "prove that the democratic myth was *no myth*."[50] Protest is viewed as a direct manifestation of learning experiences, of which school plays an important part. Kolson has argued that "campus activism is the direct result of the transmission, during the process of political socialization, of the 'participant' citizen role that is derived from a rational-activist conception of democracy."[51]

One should not be surprised, therefore, to find that students applied their hallowed democratic teachings. They felt politically efficacious, and they wanted to prove that citizens can change government policy by protesting. Indeed, in a related matter, Page found among black males in Newark, New Jersey, that "self-reported riot participants are more likely to be found among the dissident (those high on *political efficacy* but low on political trust) rather than among the alienated (those who are both distrustful and ignorant of government)."[52] Yet how students learn these democratic participatory norms is unclear. It has been well documented that the impact of high school civics courses has been minimal.[53] Merelman has concluded that the high school experience does not increase support for, or understanding of, democratic values.[54] But Grove, Remy, and Zeigler suggest that the total impact of the school's informal socialization into democratic values can have important consequences for adding to student unrest.[55] They noted: "The incongruities between the ideals of participation, critical thinking, rational inquiry, and political awareness espoused in the formal curriculum and the realities of the sociopolitical organization of schools as experienced daily by students is a potentially major factor in student dissatisfaction....If the school does not serve as a model for the values it purveys, then student unrest would seem likely to increase in scope and frequency."[56]

Another view in the social learning approach to student protest activity deals with imitation. The imitation view sees the mass media as an important political socializing agent, and it stresses the importance of peer groups for providing role models. Therefore, protest activity was just a fad, like the hoolahoop. Students imitated what they had seen others do, as reported by mass media. Besides, protesting was fun![57] The struggle was not to end the war, but rather to make the local, state, or national news. There was a sense of community among the participants, and this helped draw in many "fellow travelers." Media-created protest heroes emerged. Confrontation became ritualized. Students would select A, police would react with B, students would respond with C, and finally authorities would react with D as the camera whirled. Abbie Hoffman, Jerry Rubin, Rennie Davis, and Tom Hayden were "doing it." They provided role models of "hippie-radicals." One had to be socialized into the youth-rock-radical culture. As mass consumers of excitement, the nation's youth bought this "revolutionary" pitch much like one would buy a record album, car, or toothpaste. It was simply the case of middle-class, white kids' "perpetual struggle to ease middle-class boredom."[58] Radical politics were just something to "get into," like drugs, sex, rock music, or sports. There was no meaning other than the reinforcement of fun.

Protest activity under a social learning perspective might be explained in terms of the spread of a revolutionary consciousness in the United States, though it is not always clear who is spreading what. This revolutionary consciousness approach has many variations, like the spread of Maoist, Marxist, "New Left," Gandhian, or even Charles Reich's Con III consciousness. All variations posit a fundamental change in one's belief system through persuasion, enlightenment, stress, and logical "reasoning."

Of all the revolutionary consciousness approaches to student protest activity in the late 1960s to early 1970s, perhaps Reich's Con III approach is the most representative. He said: "There is a revolution coming. It will not be like revolutions of the past. It will originate with the individual and with culture, and it will change the political structure only as its final act. It will not require violence to succeed, and it cannot be successfully resisted by violence. This is the revolution of the new generation."[59] Reich's book categorized the three states of political and cultural consciousness. Consciousness I represented the early American tradition, complete with a sense of rugged individualism, hard work, puritan morality, and an unregulated economy. Consciousness II represented the "corporate state" mentality, with liberal reform, regulated managerial economy, the public interest, FDR New Deal, and the Kennedys being the key bywords. Consciousness III represented the new revolutionary consciousness of young people, which stressed freedom, liberation, love of the land, nonmaterialistic values, and the youth-rock culture.

Reich's book created a storm of controversy in 1970 and 1971. Critics were divided over the merits of Reich's analysis. His anatomy of the corporate state and his chapters outlining the serious problems for individuals who live in a capitalistic, technologized society are strong intellectual contributions. But his inevitable solution, a "greening" cultural revolution that would change political structures without organized political action, brought criticism from political thinkers of many different persuasions.

What develops a revolutionary consciousness for a whole generation of people? What images could possibly work together to produce Consciousness III? Reich is vague on this question. Was it a combination of Rosa Parks, affluent parents, beatniks, Lawrence Ferlinghetti, Ken Kesey, Selma, Martin Luther King, Jr., Bob Dylan and Joan Baez, freedom rides, bus boycotts, sit-ins, Stokely Carmichael, Medgar Evers, the assassination of John F. Kennedy, the Beatles, the Rolling Stones, the Berkeley free-speech movement, the peace movement, the Black Panthers, Sgt. Pepper, Jefferson Airplane, the Doors, women's liberation, Cream, Jimi Hendrix, Janis Joplin, Bobby Kennedy, Gene

McCarthy, the 1968 Democratic national convention, the
Weathermen, the Days of Rage, the Stones' 1969 tour,
Woodstock, Altamont, Kent State, Jackson State, Cambodia,
Angela Davis, the Chicago Seven, Lenny Bruce, Dick Gregory,
hippies, Attica State, May Day 1971, the war, Daniel Ellsberg,
the Berrigans, capitalism, Nixonian repression, or something
else that helped create this new national consciousness on the
Con III level? The above symbols are important in the development of so-called revolutionary consciousness, yet this approach
has serious empirical and methodological problems, for example: What is consciousness? How is it measured? How can one
test consciousness intersubjectively? What is the mix of
variables? Under what conditions? Why do some persons
develop a revolutionary consciousness while others do not?
What about the problems of reliability and validity?

Reich detailed how rock music made that great transforma-
tion during 1966-67:

1. All the separate musical traditions were brought together
   and all of the artists worked toward broader eclecticism and
   synthesis.
2. Musical groups began to use the full range of electric instruments and the technology of electronic amplifiers.
3. The music became a multimedia experience with light shows
   and dancing.
4. The groups developed their own personality and life style.
5. Musician-listener rapport was heightened by two other kinds
   of participation: many listeners played the new music
   themselves and shared the drug experience.
6. A pulsing new energy entered into all the forms of music.
7. The new music developed a remarkable complexity.
8. Not only did the groups play the new music, but they began
   composing it as well.
9. The new music achieved a height of knowledge, understanding, insight, and truth concerning the world and
   people's feelings that is greater than what other media had
   been able to express.[60]

The late Ralph J. Gleason, dean of Rolling Stone's rock critics,
felt that Reich's book was the most important piece of work ad-

dressed to the adults of this country in several years.[61] It is no wonder that Gleason would feel this way. His approach to organizing the study of rock music and society was similar to Reich's approach. Gleason felt that rock music had incredible power, and that it had great social and political import. He had long argued that rock music could be a vital force for social change. Gleason also believed in rock music's power to change attitudes. He argued that if rock could stay clear of New Left political types and big business domination, then it could be a positive sociopolitical force.[62] Gleason's "Perspective" columns were probably the most perceptive pieces written on the relationship between rock music and politics. However, when one views Gleason's pre-Reich and post-Reich positions, empirical questions arise. Have Reich and Gleason overstated rock music's power in its ability to contribute to the "greening" of America?

Garry Wills was critical of Reich's positions on the soft revolution and on the power of rock music as a political socializing agent. Wills said, "You can no more recommend that we all go out and be Bob Dylan than tell everyone to go be Michelangelo."[63] Wills claimed that it was Reich, not the radicals, who missed the point. Wills argued that Dylan did not change the world by living his own life but because he is a musical genius.[64] Wills also disagreed with Reich's notion that the most successful cooperatives today seem to be the rock groups that live and work together. Wills said: "He [Reich] offers as a model that sick world of drugs and booze and groupies, of capitalistic scrambling and recording contracts, of rock festival rip-offs. It is not a dark world for him, the world Hendrix and Joplin lived in, and died of, the world of the Woodstock con job and the Altamont murder, the world John Lennon remembers as 'constant pain.' "[65]

Ellen Willis, then rock critic for the *New Yorker*, asked the question, "Can a man who hates the juke box love the Beatles?"[66] She thought Reich's attitude toward rock was at best tiresome and at worst a prime example of upper-middle-class cultural backlash. She thought Reich could not write effectively about rock because he had no feeling for the mass culture that had spawned the music. She disagreed with Reich's contention that rock music was a triumph of art over money and human over machine. For someone to argue that rock was above the consumption ethic was nonsense. And that someone like Reich argued that "the Beatles and the Stones would never sell out" made Willis laugh. Willis suggested that perhaps Reich was guilty of over-intellectualizing rock music and was guilty of upper-middle-class bias against mass culture.[67]

R. Serge Denisoff, Bowling Green State University sociologist and editor of *Popular Music and Society* (a journal devoted to the study of popular music and its relationship to society), has written on the power of rock music. He urges students of rock music and society to chart an empirical investigation into rock's alleged power to change attitudes.[68] How does Denisoff deal with the position argued by Reich and some of his followers that rock music has great power over the young and is a positive political socializing agent that is helping to change the world for the better in the form of a "greening" America? Denisoff wants to look at the empirical evidence. He said, "Music is unquestionably a form of communication, but what is it saying and to whom?"[69] Denisoff says, "It becomes readily apparent that the mere hearing of protest song X will not turn the listener into being a supporter of X ideology or group. If this were the case the average listener to Top Forty Radio would be a Green Beret supporter of pacifist causes who takes drugs and beats up long-haired youths for opposing the Vietnam war. Such a bizarre and schizoid collection of attitudes has rarely been encountered by either social scientists or psychiatrists."[70]

Denisoff pointed out that rock music is not a collection of monolithic, hip movement songs that convey uniform values and ideology to the listener. Nor is it a simple one-way proposition from medium to listener resulting in some radical attitude change. Rock music is so diverse that the values and symbols conveyed do not form a neat ideological package. Many other dynamics are operating in rock music and its effect on the listener. Questions arise as to whether listeners even hear the lyrics and what the lyrics mean. Denisoff, of course, does not buy Reich's theories about the power of rock music to change attitudes or to help form a Consciousness III that is going to save the world. Instead, he prefers to make an empirical question of the actual power of rock music in the political socializing arena.

Michael Brown, a political scientist at California State University, who has written in the area of the "middle class young's politics of convenience," delivered a paper at the annual meeting of the Midwest Political Science Association in Chicago in 1973. Brown's paper, "Alienation among Middle Class Young: Politics, Drugs, and Ambisexualism," argued that the middle-class child or teenager leads a boring, lonely, and aimless life that had serious political implications. The world of the middle-class young was "excruciatingly homogeneous in age, social class, in color, in patterns of learning," said Brown.[71] The middle-class young had a convenient, casual, and undemanding life that was economically and physically secure and emotionally predictable.[72]

Brown characterized the 1960s as a period in which behavior was marked by a pursuit of "something to get into."[73] Though they learned the value of self-centeredness, convenience, non-accomodation, and security, the middle-class young were ripe for modes of behavior that promised quick relief from boredom while attaining values of risk, interaction, and community. Brown detailed how this group pursued political protest in the 1960s as an effort to escape their boredom and in response to their affluent alienation, which was characterized by "meaninglessness, normlessness, interpersonal estrangement, and psychic isolation."[74] The drug solution to boredom and alienation developed almost simultaneously with the rise of radical political protest in the 1960s. Brown theorized: "Clearly, middle-class drug use was more congruent with the values of the generation than political activism. In their effect, drugs are self-centered, privatistic, and a convenient mode of sensualism; being "high" justified nonaccomodation, or "doing my own thing." In relation to others, doping provided a sense of special community; identity was achievable by insignias of dress, hair, and in-group lingo. The authority risk factor was calculated, and anyone who got "busted" was either careless or stupid."[75]

Brown outlined how the young drug users and the young politicos "cross-pollinated." For various reasons both movements died out as a symbol of community and as a relief from middle-class affluent boredom and alienation. Brown suggested that the next movement in the 1970s would be an attempt by young people to "get into" ambisexualism, stating that David

Bowie had done for the ambisexual movement what the Rolling Stones and Beatles had done for drugs. Bowie and other glitter rockers have legitimized ambisexualism for masses of middle-class young, and they have provided the boundaries for the movement. Brown predicted that the ambisexualism movement, which was just beginning, would follow the same scenario as other movements. It would take shape in urban areas among more sophisticated, upper-middle-class young in their early and middle twenties.[76]

According to Brown, role models of the movement would emerge as would the lingo and behavioral characteristics. Ambisexualism would spread to surrounding middle-class suburbs and then into large and medium-sized cities. Brown concluded the paper by adding: "And so another prerogative of the intellectual upper classes and bohemian urban subcultures will be democratized, popularized, and disseminated to the bored and hungrily available middle classes, much in the fashion of drugs and radical politics. At the rate of middle-class consumption of the habits and lifestyles of existent subcultures, cultural egalitarianism is not long off. Perhaps we need a public policy of cultural ecology to protect the traditionally deviant, but picturesque, subcultures from middle-class plunder and homogenization."[77]

In another study, sociologists William Fox and James Williams found that rock music did not have a leftist or strong liberal orientation.[78] Certain political orientations of listeners are associated with musical styles, but their study found that most young people were not directly moved by the lyrics. If rock music presented the sounds of "social change" as had been argued before, this study found that it was a very faint sound.[79]

Still another approach to explaining student protest activity under the social learning perspective is "direct personal political experience." This might be compared to Abramson's "political reality" explanation of low trust and low efficacy among black school children.[80] The "direct personal political experience" approach values the power of media, events, and personal political experiences as important political socialization agents. Political socialization is viewed as a dynamic, ongoing process and not as the static world of traditional childhood socialization studies. People are continuously being socialized into and by the political system. Political learning never ceases unless the individual's mind ceases to function. Political learning and the political socialization process does not magically stop at age seventeen.

If a college student observing an antiwar rally has his head split open by a police officer, this event can be an important political socializing experience. If one's best friend dies in Indochina and the Vietnam war is perceived as worthless, this can have a radicalizing effect. Tear-gassing of demonstrators can be an important learning experience for participants and innocent bystanders. Donald Thistlethwaite has noted the effect of disruptive events like the Cambodia invasion and the Kent State killings on student attitude formation,[81] and Merelman has noted that policy thinking may be a function of "politically related stimuli alone when such stimuli are intense, politically visible, and unequivocal," rather than a function of maturation of skills in a developmental process.[82] Thus the "direct personal political experience" approach explains protest behavior as learned behavior that results from an individual's own awareness of "political reality." The political reality of elite repression and response in the late 1960s served as a socializing agent for many "fellow travelers."

The last approach under social learning theories is "rational-activist goal-directed instrumental behavior." This approach is simple and straightforward. Protest activity for some was the preferred way to reach their specified goal.[83] Behavior was goal directed and learned through past successes and failures. An individual saw successes and failures of other forms of political action and consciously chose protest activity as the best vehicle to obtain his or her goal. This is almost a Downsian[84] approach to political protest. One might conceive of "the calculus of protest" as well as a calculus of voting.[85]

CRITIQUE OF THE APPROACHES

Many of the approaches to the phenomena of student protest activity in the years 1965-1971 overlap. The approaches are not mutually exclusive; a combination of approaches would have broader explanatory power. Each approach probably explains at least some protest behavior for a selected number of protest participants.

Another problem is that the approaches do not deal with the question of the wide range of protest behavior that can be qualitatively and quantitatively different. Are the approaches trying to explain bombings, campus sit-ins, peace marches, flag burnings, ROTC takeovers, door-to-door canvassing, draft evasion, emblem wearing, or antiwar sloganeering? What kind of protest activity are the approaches trying to deal with? And the approaches do not encompass all kinds of protest behavior that were available to people from 1965 to 1971.

All the theories fail to deal with the question of the lack of protest now on college campuses, although social learning theory has a little easier time of it by claiming a "change in the environment."

Another question that divides the eight approaches into different camps is whether to pursue the question of the success of protest behavior. One group of approaches (psychoanalytic, cognitive developmental, expressive function, and imitation) would argue that the question of the success of student protest activity is irrelevant. The consequences of one's actions and eventual outcomes of protracted behavior are not questions to pursue. In psychoanalytic theory the consequences of protest behavior would not be important since the individual's behavior has been practically determined during his or her formative psychosexual development. The cognitive developmental people would be interested in establishing the stage of moral development for the individual. The imitation and the expressive function views would not pursue the question, since for them the act itself is the important focal point.

Another group of social learning approaches, civic education, revolutionary consciousness, direct personal political experience, and rational-activist, might wish to pursue the success of the antiwar movement to check environmental feedback stimuli. If one's actions are constantly failing to achieve a certain goal, then one might refrain from that kind of activity and become quiescent.

The approaches might be critiqued as follows:

1. *Psychoanalytic approach.* This approach is deterministic. It does not help us to explain why some "maladjusteds" take to the streets and others remain "in the closet" or the library. The static, subjective concepts of psychotherapy probably would tell us that somewhere around the years 1948 to 1954 there were many psychosexual maladjustments, and this statistically higher proportion of "potential deviants" could take to the streets only in the late 1960s and early 1970s. This approach does not tell us what the catalyst was or will be. Perhaps these deviants might take to the streets again in the 1980s and early 1990s when they are in their forties. Who knows?

2. *Expressive function approach.* This notion makes an important contribution in telling us that sometimes frustration can lead to aggression; it contains elements of the psychoanalytic approach. It fails, however, to help us understand why people select protest activity to release frustration. Many other ways exist to release frustration. Aggression is only one form of release. What are the goals of the participants, how are they blocked, and why do protestors feel compelled to select protest activity over some other mode of frustration release?

3. *Cognitive developmental approach.* This one has some interesting features; for example, if you were against the Vietnam war, you might be attracted by some research that showed protestors as having higher moral development than the rest of the nation. But the cognitive developmental view does not tell us why some people at a higher level of moral reasoning protest actively and others do not. It also fails to explain protest behavior by people at lower stages of moral development.

4. *Social learning approach: Civic education perspective.* This approach has some strong points, such as the internalization of the democratic myth, yet it does not tell us who internalizes and who does not. Presumably the socialization process regarding the democratic idea is fairly standard in school textbooks. But why weren't more citizens in the streets during the late 1960s and early 1970s? Students are taught not to take the law into their own hands or to break the law;

they are taught the value of citizen participation. Which values lead to what kinds of behavior?

5. *Social learning approach: Imitation view.* This view adds to our understanding of "fellow travelers" in the movement, but it does not tell us why some people selected protest activity to imitate. Why did they not imitate their parents, the U.S. Army, or the president? There are other ways to relieve "middle-class boredom." Why protest? Why was it the thing to do?

6. *Social learning approach: Revolutionary consciousness.* This view is too subjective. What is "revolutionary conscious- ness?" What are the symptoms? How does one know when one has it? Is it contagious? How does it spread? This is a never-never land that is interesting to enter, yet one doesn't leave with hard, empirical, verifiable evidence.

7. *Social learning approach: Direct personal political ex- perience.* This view is important since it sees political socialization as a dynamic ongoing process. It speaks to the possible radicalizing effects of events. However, it does not tell us which people will be affected by what events and with what consequences. If one is hit on the head by a policeman, one does not automatically become an antiwar radical. One might become a quiescent, apolitical person who wishes to avoid confrontation with police at all costs.

8. *Social learning approach: Rational-activist goal-directed instrumental behavior.* This view comes close to being a "calculus of protest" approach. It gives antiwar protestors credit for calculation and rational thought in an effort to reach their goal of ending the war. It probably can't account for the irrational behavior of some. Much of the antiwar behavior was spontaneous and in reaction to certain steps that authorities took. Much of the antiwar behavior had a strong emotional content. This approach fails to deal with these.

3/The Marijuana Policies of the United States

IN A DISCUSSION OF THE marijuana policies of the United States, it becomes necessary to develop some historical perspective. The questions that the historical survey should attempt to answer are, How was the marijuana policy formed? How did marijuana come to be outlawed? What social factors were involved? What federal agencies were involved?

After dealing with certain historical questions about the marijuana policies of the United States up to the 1950s, we can then look at the politics of marijuana in the 1970s. During that time, marijuana use became so widespread among the young, and the government's response became so harsh, that the marijuana question soon developed into a great political question.

MARIJUANA POLICIES, 1900-1950

Marijuana is a plant that has enjoyed a long and controversial relationship with humankind, especially in the Western world. Scientifically labeled *Cannabis sativa* by Linnaeus in 1753, marijuana is known throughout most of the world as Indian hemp.

Though marijuana has been used for centuries in nations such as India, Vietnam, and Mexico as a traditional social smoke, the United States has both zealously embraced and vigorously outlawed marijuana and its various products.[1]

During the American Colonial period, England looked forward to abundant yields of the valuable crop because the colonies had an ideal climate for growing hemp. Hemp was used for making rope, twine, and webbing, so the colonists grew vast amounts of it. During and after the Revolution, American farmers continued to grow hemp, especially in the Kentucky region. Of the founding fathers, only George Washington was a substantial hemp grower, though others may have dabbled in the crop. In Washington's diary there are entries that show he planted and harvested hemp, but he makes no mention of smoking it.

Some marijuana smokers like to claim that Washington, Jefferson, and Madison all smoked the Indian hemp plant after harvests, though the fact that they grew the plant does not prove they used the plant as an intoxicant. The idea that the founding fathers smoked marijuana seems implausible.

The hemp industry in the United States continued to grow, with slave labor being used to harvest the crop, until after the Civil War, but the industry was plagued by wildly fluctuating prices and great competition from the higher-quality Russian hemp.[2] With the introduction of the superior Philippine crop to the world market in the late 1800s, U.S. production entered a fatal slump that eventually saw the death of the industry here for all practical purposes. In 1940 it was estimated that Russia produced 60 percent of the world's hemp, the U.S. produced 1 percent, and the Phillipines produced most of the rest.[3]

In the United States during the period 1900-1920, there was little governmental concern over the use of the Indian hemp plant as an intoxicant. A review of the periodicals for that period shows only seven articles dealing with drugs, and only a few of those related to marijuana. In 1917, Charles B. Towns, a reporter for the *New York Times*, first noted the correlation between "war and the dope-habit." He felt that "the war...resulted in a tremendous and unnecessary increase in the use of habit forming drugs."[4] (This charge has been made during every war since World War I and especially during the Vietnam war.)

Towns was perhaps one of the first antidrug lobbyists when he went to Washington in 1917 to forcefully bring attention to the drug problem. He presented President Woodrow Wilson with facts concerning the growth of the drug habit among our troops in Europe, and he asked for a presidential drug commission and congressional legislation to solve the problem.[5]

Willard Wright, in a 1917 issue of *Literary Digest,* offered a dissenting note in the new drug controversy sweeping the nation. Wright felt that America was treating the victims of dope habits as sinners rather than as patients. He also charged Washington, D.C., specialists with being strongly influenced by the dope superstition of the era. He said, "I have yet seen no physician who has yet shown any morally degenerating action of drugs."[6] Wright's comments were significant because his was one of the few rational voices during the period of drug horror stories; that is, Wright acknowledged that literary superstitions with regard to dope often influenced policy.

Arnold Taylor, in his book on American diplomacy and the narcotics trade, deals with U.S. policy and treaty making with the nations of the world to limit traffic in hard narcotics, such as heroin, cocaine, morphine, and especially opium. From the Shanghai Opium Commission conferences of 1909, to the Hague Opium Conference in a later year, to the Geneva Opium Conference of 1924-25, Taylor examines United States drug policy making. Marijuana was hardly discussed at the world conventions. Some specialists argued that the use of marijuana was so small that it did not justify restrictive measures.[7] But the United States did succeed later, with the zealous efforts of Harry J. Anslinger, then commissioner of the Federal Narcotics Bureau. He tried to get Indian hemp on the agenda for discussion in the 1936 Conference for the Suppression of the Illicit Traffic in Dangerous Drugs at Geneva.

On the domestic front, drug legislation was centered around hard narcotics. Through revenue tactics, The Harrison Drug Act of 1914 outlawed opiate use in the United States. A 1924 act amended the Harrison act to prohibit the importation of opium to manufacture heroin. Thus by 1924 the hard-drug laws outlawing opium, cocaine, and heroin had been passed, with no great concern for the Indian hemp plant. Other drug acts followed, such as the 1929 act that set up Public Health Service hospitals for the treatment of the narcotic addicts who were shut off from the drugs by earlier acts of Congress. Another was the 1930 act that established the Bureau of Narcotics, headed by a commissioner of narcotics under the U.S. Treasury Department.[8] But until the 1930s the use of Indian hemp was not perceived to be a great enough problem to warrant any kind of legislation. Though the 1914 Harrison Act cut off opium from its addicted users, it took the United States fifteen years to establish public facilities to treat addicts like patients instead of criminals. Compared to European countries, the United States was late in setting up such facilities, even though in 1919 Joseph P. Chamberlain of the Columbia University Legislative Drafting Research Fund argued for a national policy of public care of addicts. He wrote: "The police arm of the government is striking amiss....The drug problem is a national problem, national in its scope, national in the means which must be used to meet it....No government should be satisfied in this day and generation to cut off narcotics without provision for those who will suffer by the salutary operation."[9]

With the creation of the Federal Bureau of Narcotics, staffed mostly by ex-prohibition officers, a new era in marijuana policy was ushered in. By 1930 only sixteen states had legislation on the books against marijuana, and even those laws were rarely enforced.[10] Certainly it was common knowledge that marijuana was a potent intoxicant. The states had precedent for outlawing it, but the federal government had not yet taken any stand on marijuana.

Few international studies had been done on the effects of marijuana, and certainly no American study had been done to offer scientific reason why the states should outlaw marijuana. In fact the only notable government research project on marijuana before the 1930s was the famous British Indian Hemp Commission Report of 1894. This study, conducted by British investigators in Bengal, showed that Indian hemp does not cause insanity, nor is it physically damaging or a factor in crime. The researchers concluded that moderate use of the drug produces no moral injury whatsoever, and moderation is usually the rule for most marijuana users.[11]

Before 1936, when the Federal Bureau of Narcotics became involved in an intensive campaign to alert the public to the dangers of marijuana, a number of studies in the United States tended to support the findings of the Indian Hemp Commission. The physiological and psychological effects of marijuana smoking by U.S. soldiers stationed in Panama were reported in the Panama Canal Zone Governor's Report (1933), which stated that marijuana was not habit forming nor did it cause any maladjustment in the user.[12] In 1934, W. Bromberg published the results of his psychiatric study of convicted marijuana smokers in New York; he found that there was no relationship between marijuana smoking and crime, nor was marijuana viewed to be habit-forming.[13]

The repeal of the 1919 Volstead Act in 1933 was an important event in the history of marijuana policy. The repeal of prohibition allowed agents such as H. J. Anslinger to devote their time to stopping narcotics in the United States. It also meant that liquor manufacturers who looked forward to a new era of prosperity would step up pressures to prohibit a cheap, popular intoxicant like marijuana from taking business away from their industry.[14]

Under the direction of Commissioner Anslinger, the Federal Bureau of Narcotics spearheaded an educational campaign to alert the American public to the dangers of marijuana. Articles began appearing in scientific journals about these dangers. One article that appeared in a 1936 *Scientific American* claimed marijuana was menacing American youth by addiction.[15] Horror stories appeared about the ugly crimes that marijuana users had purportedly committed, but most of the information for these stories was provided by the bureau itself. In an effort to prepare the national climate for some type of marijuana legislation, Anslinger continued to preach the evils of the drug.

On the international level, Anslinger brought up marijuana for discussion at the Conference for the Suppression of the Illicit Traffic in Dangerous Drugs in Geneva in 1936; this was a personal triumph of sorts.[16] Domestically, Anslinger had prepared the way for a national outcry against marijuana. Only a few periodicals remained moderate in the ensuing debate. One that maintained its balance during the Anslingerian attacks on marijuana was *Literary Digest*, which in 1936 claimed marijuana was not a habit-forming drug.[17]

The Anslinger campaign against marijuana culminated in the Marijuana Tax Act of 1937. Anslinger, in his book *The Murderers*, gives a fair account of the campaign against marijuana. He wrote: "As the marijuana situation grew worse, I knew action had to be taken to get proper control legislation passed. By 1937, under my direction, the bureau launched two important steps. First, a legislative plan to seek from Congress a new law that would place marijuana and its distribution directly under federal control. Second, on radio and at major forums, such as that presented annually by the *New York Herald Tribune*, I told the story of this evil weed of the fields and riverbeds and roadsides. I wrote articles for magazines; our agents gave hundreds of lectures to parents, educators, social and civic leaders. In network broadcasts I reported on the growing list of crimes, including murder and rape. I described the nature of marijuana and its close kinship to hashish. I continued to hammer at the facts....I believe we did a thorough job, for the public was alerted, and laws to protect them were passed, both nationally and at the state level. We also brought under control the wild growing marijuana in this country."[18]

Indeed, Anslinger did do a thorough job, for it was mainly through his efforts that the 1937 marijuana act was passed. The hearings before the House Committee on Ways and Means lasted only five days, with very little empirical evidence introduced that supported the later legislative judgment. In fact, the primary function of the hearing was to titillate the legislators with horror stories.[19] No medical, scientific, or sociological evidence was sought or heard, and no alternatives to criminalizing the users were considered. Major attention was given to the birdseed and paint industries, which needed access to the hemp plant.[20] Anslinger was the star witness at the House hearings as he told how marijuana caused murder, rape, and insanity. One district attorney told how marijuana was an aphrodisiac that led to impotence, while another told of several criminals he had prosecuted who did not remember whether or not they had committed the crime because they were on marijuana.

The House committee amended the bill so that all industries that needed to use the hemp plant would not be affected by the tax act, and then they called for the last witness, Dr. William C. Woodward, legislative counsel for the American Medical Association. Woodward opposed the bill on several counts, one being that all previous testimony was based primarily on hearsay evidence. This charge apparently irked the committee members who had anticipated little opposition to their efforts. The members challenged his credibility and castigated him for not cooperating. They reminded the doctor of the previous horror stories that had been relayed to the committee and advised the top-rated AMA counsel, "If you want to advise us on legislation, you ought to come here with some constructive proposals, rather than criticism, rather than trying to throw obstacles in the way of something the federal government is trying to do."[21]

The committee quickly approved the legislation, and the House readily agreed with the committee's report. The Senate hearings showed even less debate over the scientific questions about marijuana, and Anslinger was again the star witness as he reiterated his horror stories about the crimes caused by marijuana. The Senate quickly followed suit, and the Marijuana Tax Act of 1937 became a reality.

The Marijuana Tax Act was a revenue act that required all transfers of marijuana to be accompanied by a Treasury Department order form. The purchaser had to pay $100 on every ounce of marijuana purchased, which made it economically impossible for anyone to buy an ounce of marijuana. Thus marijuana per se was not outlawed by federal law, but it became very costly to buy it.[22]

Anslinger was not content with his federal victory and continued to bombard the print media with his marijuana horror stories. In perhaps the classic marijuana attack, Anslinger, in a 1938 issue of *Reader's Digest*, called marijuana a "murderer" and "more dangerous than a coiled rattlesnake." He wrote, "How many murders, suicides, robberies, and maniacal deeds it causes each year, especially among the young, can only be conjectured."[23] He claimed marijuana made users go insane. He partly blamed musicians for the spread of the intoxicant, and he

especially disliked Cab Calloway's song about the "reefer man."
He incorrectly labeled marijuana a "narcotic," and he wanted
everyone to know that marijuana brought insanity and disgrace
upon the user. He wrote: "The girl who decides suddenly to elope
with a boy she did not even know a few hours before, does so,
with the confident belief that this is a thoroughly logical action
without the slightest possibility of disastrous consequences....
Everything no matter how insane becomes plausible."[24]

Anslinger also supplied "data" for other magazine articles,
and Scientific American in 1938 related how Anslinger felt marijuana was more dangerous than heroin or cocaine. He said he
was surprised to see some authorities minimizing the dangers of
marijuana. He felt that if these experts would only check out
bureau files, they would quickly see that the drug was causing
murder, assault, rape, physical demoralization, and mental
breakdown. Anslinger also talked of "the evil instincts" that the
drug brought to the surface.[25]

In Science News Letter, later in 1938, marijuana was seen as
an epidemic among the idle young. Morals were lowered by the
drug, thus producing spontaneous acts of violence, according to
the article, which had a largely Anslingerian influence.[26] Indeed,
Anslinger had sold the entire nation on the evils of marijuana, or
so it seemed.

In 1938, Mayor Fiorello La Guardia of New York set up a
distinguished team of scientists to study the medical, psychological, and sociological aspects of marijuana use in New York
City. The findings were published in 1944, and though the study
was the most comprehensive and reliable American study yet
undertaken on marijuana, the public largely disregarded the
controversial conclusions.[27] The mayor's committee found that
marijuana smoking does not lead directly to mental or physical
deterioration, does not develop addiction or tolerance as is
characteristic of hard drugs, and is not a direct causal factor in
sexual or criminal misconduct.[28]

Anslinger, of course, strongly disagreed with the La Guardia
Report and called the findings unscientific. The American
Medical Journal of the American Medical Association in 1942
suggested, after they caught wind of a few of the early La Guardia findings, that the study was a careful one that showed possi-

ble therapeutic uses for marijuana. But after receiving and publishing letters from Anslinger in 1943 and from R. J. Bouquet, an expert on the Narcotics Commission of the League of Nations, in 1944, both of which attacked the La Guardia Report, the AMA, in a 1945 editorial, reversed its earlier view of the study and said that it was a "thoroughly unscientific" report that "drew sweeping conclusions" that "minimized the harmfulness of marijuana."[29] The AMA said it felt that the La Guardia statement had already done significant public damage.

Anslinger, in *The Murderers,* claimed that the La Guardia report did untold harm to the nation. He felt that the narcotics branch of the underworld was given a new lift by the publication of the report after his bureau had strived so hard to keep marijuana in its prohibited place. He wrote: "There can be no doubt of the damage done by the report. Syndicate lawyers and spokesmen leaped upon its giddy sociology and medical mumbo-jumbo, cited it in court cases, tried to spread the idea that the report had brought marijuana back into the folds of good society with the full pardon and a slap on the back from the medical profession.... The lies continued to spread. They cropped up on panel discussions, in public addresses by seemingly informed individuals. They helped once again, in a new and profitable direction, to bewilder the public and make it unsure of its own judgments."[30]

While the controversy about the effects of marijuana was raging on the home front, the United States was engaged in World War II. The war brought with it the usual increase in drug use among American soldiers. But it also brought on another important factor in the history of American marijuana policy. The Philippines were shut off from trading with the United States, and America's hemp supply was dwindling. The United States started subsidizing the growing of Indian hemp by midwestern farmers, which is why marijuana can be found growing today in the Midwest, especially in Indiana. The war also produced a U.S. Army report on marijuana smoking.[31]

Anslinger continued to dominate the marijuana policy of the United States through the 1950s and, at the end of the "assassin" period in marijuana policy (1900-1950), the Anslingerian ideology seemed well established. Earl Wilson, in an article in *Collier's*, called the La Guardia report "the work of amateur experts." Wilson was appalled by the public's ignorance of the "evils" of marijuana, since the Federal Narcotic Bureau, under Anslinger's command, had been hammering away for years to educate the public. Wilson agreed with Anslinger's view that marijuana leads to hard drugs. Wilson said, "It is a simple hop, skip, and jump from marijuana to cocaine, then to morphine, then to heroin."[32] Colonel Garland H. Williams, head of the New York office of the Federal Narcotics Bureau, also agreed with Anslingerian ideology toward marijuana and added: "Even sex does not satisfy the abnormal urges induced by marijuana. There is still the necessity for further excitement, more emotional release. That is when guns are grabbed, knives waved, and razors swung. All this is a marijuana user's idea of what is normal."[33]

In 1952, Dr. Victor Vogel, director of the Federal Narcotics Hospital at Lexington, Kentucky, attacked those few defendents of marijuana who were arguing that it was less harmful or habitual than tobacco smoking or coffee drinking. He said, "Marijuana leads to heroin. Let's face facts. All teen-age addicts at Lexington had first smoked marijuana for a period before becoming curious [as] to the effects of heroin. Coffee, soft drinks, and tobacco don't lead to heroin use by teen-agers, but marijuana does."[34]

Thus the "assassin" period in American marijuana policy ended with Anslingerian ideology almost single-handedly shaping policy, even though there were many scientific reports that refuted most, if not all, of Anslinger's positions on marijuana. The stage was set for the next era of marijuana policy, the 1960s.

MARIJUANA IN THE 1960S

The decade of the 1960s brought the issue of marijuana to the national forefront once again, but this time it had new sociological and political implications. No longer was marijuana use confined to black, Puerto Rican, or Mexican communities. Its use was widespread among white, middle-class youths who were creating a new lifestyle. These young people, who placed great emphasis on the concept of liberation and the need for more choices in one's everyday existence, came to see the marijuana laws as hypocritical. In the era of Vietnam, the Beatles, the Rolling Stones, the antiwar movement, and "Black Power," the government's stand on marijuana was viewed as an example of the hypocrisy of federal, state, and local decision-makers. At a time when many young people lacked faith or respect for the democratic process in America the marijuana laws were seen as attempts by the "establishment" to harass and control culture and lifestyle. Many young people questioned the government's basic credibility and found it lacking. They felt that the American corporate state was killing and burning in Vietnam and that the environment at home was being destroyed by government and business "gone mad." Efforts to peacefully change the system were met with police-state repression, as many young activists perceived the situation, for example, the 1968 Democratic convention in Chicago, the government's war against the Black Panther party leadership, the Kent State and Jackson State killings in 1970. It was also a time for marijuana arrests.

The issue no longer involved the use of marijuana and its consequences, but rather the kind of people who were using it. If "hippies," "yippies," "long hairs," "freaks," and "rock musicians" were viewed by government officials as "bad," then the intoxicant that they used must also be bad. Grinspoon offers reasons why the marijuana issue for most government officials and parents was a "campaign against the drug." He writes: "Closely related to this type of reaction is the mechanism of projection.... Thus parents are frequently overly concerned about the alleged aphrodisiac properties of marijuana, and some of the questions they most frequently ask suggest an underlying fantasy that if their children use it, they will become sexually promiscuous.... There is a widespread shared fantasy that cannabis use causes loss of self-control and the emergence of primitive impulses."[35]

Another probable reason why the campaign against marijuana grew in intensity was covert racism. Grinspoon points out that until the 1960s marijuana was primarily used in the ghettos

by nonwhites. One cannot avoid questioning to what extent marijuana has been viewed as the nonwhite drug that is rapidly in-
vading the white community.[36]

Charles Reich, in *Greening of America,* points out that marijuana in a less uptight society would be a "harmless high," but in
the American corporate society where everyone must fit into a
certain systematized mold, marijuana becomes the enemy. "In a
society that keeps its citizens within a closed system of thought,
that depends so much on systematic indoctrination, and an imposed consciousness, marijuana is a maker of revolution, a
truth-serum," maintains Reich.[37] He writes: "Because it [mari-
juana] concentrates on 'nowness' as reality, it takes people outside the enclosed system, releases them from domination of their
thought, and makes unreal what society takes seriously: time,
schedules, rational connections, competition, anger, excellence,
authority, private property, law, status, the primacy of state, the
standards imposed by other people and by society. It is a truth-
serum that repeals false consciousness."[38]

Reich feels that there is a connection between marijuana use
and a new kind of political consciousness. He argues that
because of the state's absurd marijuana policy in the 1960s,
even "straight" college students could see through the government's hypocrisy to the point of becoming politically aware, in
some sense. Reich states: "Suppose that a 'straight' college
athlete, never interested in politics, tries marijuana. It will in-
evitably lead him to political and ideological concerns. Finding
that the drug is comparatively harmless but nevertheless illegal,
his credulity about laws will be strained. Realizing that the far
more harmful substances are legal, such as tobacco, alcohol,
and various nonprescription drugs, he will begin to see that ban-
ning marijuana presents an ideological rather than a scientific
question. Seeing that alcohol and tobacco yield huge profits to industry and are pressed on people by high-pressure advertising
that insists they are 'good' for you, he may draw some general
conclusions about profits, morality, and power in the corporate
state."[39]

With the 1960s bringing on new political implications of marijuana use, the federal government's response was, for the most
part, tougher enforcement of existing harsh laws. The scientific

and medical communities still debated the effects of marijuana in the 1960s, and top legal minds in the country debated whether or not marijuana should be legalized.

The crackdown arrests and tactics of the state in regard to marijuana use was functional in that it conveyed to parents that something was being done to end the use of marijuana by their children.[40] Erich Goode, in "Marijuana and the Politics of Reality," sees the marijuana crackdown in the 1960s as repression against a symbol. He writes: "Marijuana can be thought of as kind of a symbol for a complex of other positions, beliefs, and activities which are correlated with and compatible with its use. In other words, those who disapprove of marijuana use often feel that he who smokes must, of necessity, also be a political radical, engage in 'loose' (from his point of view) sexual practices, and have a somewhat dim view of patriotism."[41]

H. J. Anslinger testified before a House subcommittee in 1960 that stricter penalties should be in order for marijuana users because marijuana leads to heroin. Thus, since the passage of the Marijuana Tax Act, the properties of the drug had drastically changed in the eyes of the U.S. Commissioner of Narcotics without the benefits of minimal government research into the actual properties of the drug.[42]

In 1962, the White House Conference on Narcotic and Drug Abuse was held, the members suggesting that "the hazards of marijuana per se have been exaggerated and the long criminal sentences imposed on an occasional user or possessor of the drug are in poor social perspective."[43] In 1967, Lyndon Johnson's Commission on Law Enforcement and the Administration of Justice took a similar view, recommending more flexible penalties. Evidently, no one heard the results because the commission was not heeded. More significantly, for the first time, an arm of the U.S. government admitted that marijuana had nothing in common with true narcotics or opiates.[44]

Dr. James L. Goddard, then head of the Food and Drug Administration, was an unlikely defender of marijuana when he argued in 1966 that marijuana penalties were too severe. He felt marijuana in some sense was not any more harmful than alcohol, and he called for easing of the marijuana penalties.[45] Another state official who spoke at the same conference was Dr. Donald

Louria, a New York state councilman on drugs, who felt that the
government must legally make the distinction between marijuana, a mild hallucinogen, and heroin, a hard narcotic, since
both had been classified as narcotics by the federal government.[46]

There was no major change in government policy toward
marijuana despite the fact that more and more studies were pop-
ping up to show that the drug was not addictive, nor did it cause
insanity, crime, or immoral acts. A. T. Weil presented a monu-
mental and exhaustive study in 1969 about the physiological effects of marijuana, finding the drug to be relatively harmless as
compared to alcohol. But others in high medical and government
positions criticized the Weil study by saying, "A. T. Weil only
tested effects of a small dose of marijuana. We need more
evidence before we can say it is safe."[47]

President Richard Nixon brought forward a "new" marijuana
plan in October 1969, which brought no real shift in marijuana
policy. He asked for lesser penalties for possession and stricter
penalties for sellers of marijuana, since most of the marijuana
sentences in this country had been very harsh. Nixon also asked
for legislation that would make a clear legal distinction between
marijuana and hard narcotics, since they both fell under the
same legal heading; yet he still asked for some kind of punishment for the use of marijuana.[48] When Roger O. Egeberg, assistant secretary of Health, Education and Welfare, outlined the
Nixon plan to the press, he said that marijuana was not addict-
ing, nor was it narcotic. "Marijuana use is said to lead to the use
of more dangerous drugs, such as heroin, yet there is no scientific evidence to demonstrate that the use of marijuana in itself
predisposes an individual to progress to 'hard' drugs."[49]

Thus a government official publicly denied the Anslingerian
notion that marijuana leads to hard drugs, a thought that was
posited many times throughout the 1960s by the Federal Narcotics Bureau.

Despite arguing against many of the myths about marijuana,
Egeberg concluded his press conference with a statement that
summed up the federal government's position on marijuana:
"Don't get us wrong! The fact that the drug has been demon-
strated to be a relatively mild hallucinogen and intoxicant does

not in my mind justify or excuse its widening use among young people of this country!"[50] Perhaps, as H. L. Mencken has noted on the attitude of puritanism, Nixon and Egeberg were plagued "with the haunting fear that someone, somewhere, may be happy."

With pressures mounting in many scientific quarters for a change in our country's outmoded marijuana policies (even anthropologist Margaret Mead testified before a congressional committee that "marijuana is less harmful than cigarettes or alcohol and it should be legalized"[51]), President Nixon set up a commission to study the effects of marijuana.[52] Research was done by the National Institute of Mental Health to find out what the intoxicant does to the human body. Its work was completed by the end of 1972, though President Nixon stated that the results of this study would in no way change his position toward marijuana. Thus the commission's stand in favor of decriminalization had no impact. In the 1970s it was still illegal to possess marijuana except in Alaska and California.

ROCK AND DRUGS

One theory about popular culture argues that like a hypodermic needle, rock music can change people's attitudes with just one fix. There is little evidence to indicate that a one-dose hearing of a rock song directly leads someone to take marijuana, LSD, heroin, or cocaine. Drug usage is a complicated phenomenon. People take drugs when they are available for particular reasons, such as pleasure, to ease pain, or to imitate friends, and not necessarily because John Lennon did it. To argue that rock music created the drug society that we have today would be a misstatement.

Although rock music does not make an individual select a drug, it has helped advertise the drug life style. When rock stars such as Gregg Allman, Eric Clapton, and Keith Richards openly talk about their heroin use, the drug culture becomes closely related to the rock culture. When the New Riders of the Purple Sage sing "Panama Red" or when Eric Clapton sings "Cocaine," one cannot argue that these songs hurt the sale of drugs. The list of rock stars who died of drug overdoses and related circumstances carries names like Janis Joplin, Jimi Hendrix, Gram

Parsons, Keith Moon, Sid Vicious, and Elvis Presley. The list of rock stars who have tried drugs would by some estimates contain the names of about 90 percent of all rock stars today.

This is not to serve as an indictment of rock music but as acknowledgment that rock culture helped spread the drug culture. To be sure, the Central Intelligence Agency in the 1950s and early 1960s perfected and introduced LSD in their testing, but it was rock culture that helped spread the notion of LSD to the people. Psychedelic music, which later led to psychedelic advertising within popular culture, spoke of the good life to be found in psychedelics and hallucinogenic drugs. Jimi Hendrix, the Jefferson Airplane, Iron Butterfly, the Doors, the Grateful Dead, John Lennon, Cream, and Vanilla Fudge, among others, all helped spread propaganda that favored psychedelics. Again, this did not directly cause people to drop acid in the 1960s, but it certainly didn't discourage it. Whether the chemicals were "good" or "bad" is a scientific (and at times a value) question, but it would be absurd to maintain that rock music did not promote the use of drugs in the 1960s and 1970s. Rock music, like other art forms, does at times influence rather than reflect life. In this case, some rock stars gave free personal endorsements for a product within popular culture, and those products were marijuana, cocaine, LSD, and heroin.

4/ Rock Music and Political Attitudes

THE PRAISES OF ROCK MUSIC as a political socializing agent have been outlined by Charles Reich, Ralph Gleason, and others. The elites and critics on the right have based many of their fears about rock on the assumption that rock music could subvert the political order through its powerful political socializing abilities. But the validity of both assumptions should be tested empirically to find out how well rock music has acted as such an agent.

Political socialization deals with how individuals learn attitudes, beliefs, and values toward political objects. Political socialization studies also deal with how individuals learn patterns of political behavior. Fred Greenstein has defined political socialization as "all political learning, formal and informal, deliberate and unplanned, at every stage of the life cycle, including not only explicitly political learning but also nominally nonpolitical learning that affects political behavior, such as learning of relevant social attitudes and the acquisition of politically relevant personality characteristics."[1] But Gabriel Almond, one of the pioneers in political socialization studies, has defined political socialization as "the process of induction into the political culture. Its end product is a set of attitudes, cognitions, value standards, and feelings toward the political system, its various roles, and incumbents."[2] Greenstein has set the pace for the study of political socialization at the individual level of political behavior, and Almond's approach deals with a nation's political culture and takes a systemic approach.

Most political socialization studies that have centered on individual political orientations and activities of political socializing agents have proclaimed the family as the most important attitude-shaping agent with which the individual comes into contact. The family transmits the general norms of the American political culture, it is argued. School is the institution that is ranked second in importance, although some political scientists dissent from that view and rank schools ahead of the family in transmitting the norms of the American political culture. But other factors enter into the equation, such as a person's social class, ethnicity, or residency.

Political socialization is a process that continues throughout one's life, and political scientists have begun to study other aspects in the political socialization process to determine their impact upon political learning. Direct personal political experiences shape one's view of the political system. Peer groups can also help shape political attitudes. Mass media transmission of political ideas and values can play an important role. The mass media have often been labeled as a proximate factor in the political socialization process, but few political scientists have studied the impact of mass media on a child's political socialization. Margaret Conway and Frank Feigart have noted that "little research has examined directly the relationship between children's consumption of various mass media of communications and their political orientations."[3]

The mass media's role as political socializing agent has often been dismissed because some studies have shown that the media primarily reinforce previously existing attitudes, opinions, and values. The psychological phenomena of selective perception and selective retention usually occurs. People digest political information that is harmonious with their biases and value structures. Studies have shown that communication is a two-step flow process from medium to "opinion leader"[4] and then to the mass public after the message is filtered through the "opinion leader." This process dilutes the impact of mass media on potential attitude change and in the political socialization process.

When one studies the mass media to analyze their effect on political attitude change, one notes that a political message must be sent, received, and stored.[5] The questions can be asked: Who is sending what message to whom? What is the message saying, and Is the message understood by the listener? Is there an attitude change? Is it lasting? Does this new attitude change lead to some new political behavior?

Robert Levine has noted that greater discrepancies in the political socialization process are more likely to occur in a system that has many different socializing agents at work.[6] In a political system like that of the United States, which has a well-developed economy and technological capacities, there are many agents at work in the political socialization process.

The effects of television and newspapers have been studied by some political scientists, while other areas, such as commercial films and rock music, have been neglected for a number of reasons. They have been viewed as entertainment media that do not overtly communicate political messages or propagandize. Scholars have also stayed away from these areas because of the difficulty in gaining accurate data and because work in film and rock analysis has tended to be too subjective.

But a few social scientists recently have ventured into the area of rock music. Paul Hirsch has examined four approaches to the study of popular music with regard to its sociological and psychological effects. Hirsch has examined content analysis and the functional approach to mass media, the impact of popular music on its audience, the impact of technological change on mass media programming, and the organizational analysis of entertainment industries.[7]

Hirsch noted the changing character of American popular songs as revealed through content analysis of themes over a certain time period. In the 1950s and early 1960s, most of the popular songs contained lyrics and themes that related to courtship. In the late 1960s and early 1970s, courtship themes diminished slightly, and songs labeled as "protest songs" were

on the increase. T. Horton had found that 83 percent of the lyrics
he studied from the top hits of 1955 contained themes that dealt
with boy-girl relationships.[8] However, sociologist James Carey
found that themes of boy-girl relationships had dropped to 65
percent in his content analysis of rock 'n' roll lyrics in 1966.[9]
About the increase in the number of themes unrelated to love
and courtship, Hirsch said: "Many of these hit songs contained
lyrics which condemned war, acknowledged drug use, or other-
wise challenged the status quo. The pattern of courtship, ideal-
ized in the remaining 70 percent, is no longer one to which a majority of adults would likely subscribe (e.g., it is more physical,
less romantic, less permanent)."[10] Carey said, "The fact that
there is a distinctive set of beliefs associated with the large proportion of 1966 lyrics may reflect the growing dissatisfaction
among younger people who constitute the audience of the new
lyrics, or it may simply reflect a change in those who write
them."[11]

R. Serge Denisoff has done some work in attempting to gauge
the power of rock music as a political socializing agent and attitude changer. In 1965, a pessimistic, nihilistic warning from
nineteen-year-old songwriter P. F. Sloan, called "Eve of Destruction," became the number-one selling record in the country.[12] It
was sung and shouted by Barry McGuire, a former member of
the New Christy Minstrels. Denisoff found that only 36 percent
of his sample interpreted the lyrics to "Eve of Destruction" in the
composers' terms and only 37 percent could express some of the
sentiments of the song after repeated listening; but he also found
that 23 percent entirely misconstrued the intent of the lyric.[13]
Denisoff interviewed 180 students while "Eve of Destruction"
was riding high on the charts. He found that 44 percent approved of the song while 39 percent did not approve, and that 24
percent would dance to the song whereas 62 percent said they
would not dance to the song.[14] Denisoff concluded after his
research: "It would appear that the protest song is primarily
seen as an entertainment item rather than one of political
significance.... In sum protest on the Top Forty reaches a large
audience. Once the message has been received, it is subjected to
a number of responses, only a minority of which are affirmative.
The opinion formation function of protest songs on the Top Forty

remains unsubstantiated with the burden of proof still in the hands of the advocates of 'music is a weapon.' "[15]

Paul Hirsch pointed out that the analysts of popular music who subscribe to the "hypodermic needle" theory (instant attitude change after one song listening) base their positions on the following assumptions: the values expressed in the song are clear to a majority of listeners; the values are subscribed to by a large proportion of listeners; and the values are likely to influence the attitudes and behavior of the uncommitted.[16]

But these assumptions do not have empirical verification. Hirsch wrote, "Most teenagers are attracted to popular records more by their overall sound and beat, or to the performing group, than by their verbal content. Systemic social research has yet to demonstrate any effects of popular song lyrics upon their listeners."[17] In a study by Hirsch and Robinson using 1,200 students from selected Michigan high schools, fewer than 30 percent were able to correctly identify the "message" allegedly contained in four controversial popular "protest" song lyrics.[18] More than 70 percent of the respondents could not identify the reference to drugs, sex, or politics when Hirsch and Robinson asked them to interpret the meanings of songs that Hirsch and Robinson believed said a great deal about those subjects.[19]

Stephen Levine examined political socialization, student radicalism, and American political science in 1971. He felt existing socialization theory neglected to incorporate theories of personality development and to understand the radicalization of students in the late 1960s and early 1970s. He argued that the political implications in art, literature, and especially music were significant in the socialization process.[20] In one experiment there was a relationship between political radicalism and familiarity with folksinger Phil Ochs.

The weight of the existing empirical evidence suggests that rock music has no mystical power that can make people change their basic political values or orientations. Rock music cannot be said to be a primary political socializing agent, but it can in some instances act to persuade people who have no positions at all on various political issues. Even though rock is not a primary force in the political socialization process, it should not be dismissed lightly, for the rock industry quickly became the number-one entertainment medium and surpassed the film industry in gross profits per year. The findings so far have been against the power of music to change attitudes or to form new political orientations. But these findings and research have only begun. New research designs are needed to gauge whether certain rock songs, performed by certain rock artists, affect certain people. The effect of rock music, in combination with other political socializing forces such as political films, has not been researched. Under what circumstances, if any, are certain people susceptible to propaganda in the form of a political rock song? Must the song relate to a person's own political experience or value system? Do rock songs only reinforce previously existing attitudes? These questions and others are to be answered before one can accurately portray the capabilities of rock music as a socializing agent or as an attitude changer.

YOU ARE WHAT YOU BOOGIE TO

Only recently have social scientists begun asking questions about how clearly musical tastes and preferences can be predicted based on a knowledge of background variables. A few social scientists have studied musical taste in terms of social background, while others have studied musical taste and its relationship to certain personality characteristics. But for the most part, this kind of investigation is relatively new.

Karl Schuessler, one of the great statisticians in social science, was also interested in social background and musical taste. In a study conducted in Evansville, Indiana, Schuessler found that one's socioeconomic position operates to channel experiences "in such a way that a given individual tends to form a favorable attitude toward certain kinds of music and an unfavorable attitude towards other kinds."[21] Schuessler also found:

1. Musical taste is conditioned by persistent biases or attitudes, which in turn reflect the differentiating force of occupation, age, and sex on cultural experience.
2. The fact that musical preferences exhibit consensus confirms the sociological view that musical taste is socially controlled and opposes the commonsense formula that "there is no accounting for taste."

3. The findings on familiarity are consistent with the sociological generalization that people tend to be ethnocentric about familiar stimuli. Although continuous exposure to a particular kind of music does not necessarily lead to a favorable attitude toward such music, it appears that isolation usually leads to a negative judgment.

4. The results of the study indicate finally that generalizations about aesthetic judgments, in general, and musical taste, in particular, must take into account the specific cultural background of the group or of the individual.[22]

David Voelker has done some work with rock groups and their relationship to selected personality characteristics. Using one hundred respondents in Ohio, Voelker found that marijuana use positively correlated with rock groups Jethro Tull, Spooky Tooth, Fleetwood Mac, Jimi Hendrix, and the Grateful Dead.[23] Grass smoking negatively correlated with groups like Creedence Clearwater Revival, Three Dog Night, Chicago, and the Carpenters. All the rock groups in Voelker's small, unscientific sample correlated with the political left except for the Carpenters, who correlated with the political right.[24] Voelker found, "People who consider themselves 'radical' enjoy Hot Tuna and Pink Floyd, but turn up their noses to Paul McCartney and the Carpenters."[25] Groups such as Chicago, Guess Who, Carpenters, and Three Dog Night related positively to religion in Voelker's study. He also found that the Grateful Dead correlated negatively with the statement, "A good sex life is of great importance to me."[26] This finding can easily be disputed, though, by John Mood who often said that people he knew would have sex only when "Turn on Your Love Light" by the Dead was playing.[27]

In order to determine the relationships between a person's political attitudes and his or her favorite rock groups, two studies were conducted. Students at Ball State University and Indiana University were interviewed in 1973 and 1974 (during the Watergate era); then students were interviewed in December 1979 at Fairfield University, Connecticut, for the second study. Both studies were revealing.

THE FIRST STUDY

At Ball State, 115 students were interviewed and at Indiana University 230 students were interviewed, to form a combined sample of 345 respondents. All the interviews were completed within nine months from May 1973 through January 1974.

Students were first asked to categorize themselves on questions concerning their sex, political party identification, political ideology, and age. Then fifty to sixty political symbols were read aloud, and students were asked to translate their "feelings" into a numerical indicator from 1 to 10. For example, if the word *democracy* was said and the student responded positively to the word and its image, the highest response would be a 10. If a student was repulsed by the word, a response of 1 would be appropriate. Responses of 4, 5, and 6 to a political symbol would be considered neutral.

Next, students were asked to respond yes or no to standard poll-type questions on Watergate and related matters. The next set of questions dealt with behavior, such as drug use and hours per week that each student listened to rock music. Finally, students were asked whom they supported in the 1972 presidential election and, most importantly, they were asked to name their favorite rock groups. The responses were cross-tabulated with the favored rock groups to get an idea of what type of political attitudes correlated with which rock groups.

If we overlook a number of methodological objections to the research (e.g., the difficulty a respondent has in translating a feeling into a number, what the number indicates, the problems of combining Ball State and Indiana University samples, the validity of the responses, the reliability of the measuring devices, and so on) the tentative findings are quite interesting. The purpose of the research was to show a connection between musical tastes and political attitudes, but more importantly this study found out what political attitudes are held by the fans of a number of top rock artists and groups.

The top eighteen artists or groups were selected so that cross tabulations of their fans' political attitudes could be made, since these groups had at least twenty fans each. The groups include the Beatles, Moody Blues, Rolling Stones, Carpenters, Led Zeppelin, Yes, Allman Brothers Band, Chicago, Crosby, Stills, Nash, and Young, Elton John, Deep Purple, Pink Floyd, Who, Carly Simon, Joni Mitchell, Carole King, Jethro Tull, Bob Dylan, Alice Cooper, and Cat Stevens. All other groups or individuals did not have enough fans to make their data worthwhile. The findings were as follows:

SEX

The groups that had a disproportionate amount of female support (40 percent of the total sample was female) were the Carpenters (83 percent), Chicago (68 percent), the female singers (60 percent), Elton John (57 percent), and Cat Stevens (55 percent). The groups that had a disproportionate amount of male support were Who (85 percent), Allmans (84 percent), Yes (80 percent), Pink Floyd (78 percent), and of course the sexist Rolling Stones (74 percent).

REPUBLICAN SUPPORT

Twenty-five percent of the total sample considered themselves Republican. Groups that had relatively high percentages of Republican support were Elton John (46 percent), Pink Floyd (44 percent), Alice Cooper (40 percent), Carpenters (40 percent), and Beatles (37 percent). Groups that Republicans were not so interested in were Led Zeppelin (10 percent), Allmans (11 percent), Dylan (14 percent), and Crosby, Stills, Nash, and Young (14 percent).

DEMOCRATIC SUPPORT

Thirty-six percent of the total sample were Democrats. Jethro Tull (55 percent) and the Rolling Stones (51 percent) were the groups that had the most fans who claimed to be Democrats. On the other side, Pink Floyd had 11 percent of the fans who claimed to be Democrats, and the Carpenters ranked last at 0 percent.

INDEPENDENT SUPPORT

Thirty-nine percent of the total sample were independents. The Carpenters had the most independent support (60 percent), followed by the Who (56 percent) and Dylan (55 percent). Jethro Tull had the lowest amount of independent support (15 percent.)

IDEOLOGIES

A most remarkable finding was that Alice Cooper had the most conservative supporters (33 percent), and only 11 percent of the total sample considered themselves conservatives on most political issues. Following Alice with the most conservative supporters were the Carpenters (17 percent). Cat Stevens, Deep Purple, Pink Floyd, Crosby, Stills, Nash and Young, and the Allman Brothers Band did not have even one fan who considered himself conservative. Eighty-three percent of the Carpenters' fans considered themselves politically middle of the road, and only 43 percent of the total sample were middle-roaders. Thus all the Carpenters' fans were subsumed under the two political categories of conservative or middle of the road. Chicago had the second highest middle-of-the-road support at 68 percent, and Jethro Tull had the lowest at 25 percent.

The Allman Brothers Band had the most liberal support at 67 percent, followed by the Rolling Stones (60 percent), with the total sample size of liberals being 43 percent. The Carpenters had no liberal support, and the next lowest percent of liberal support came from Chicago fans, only 21 percent of whom considered themselves liberal. Very few groups had any radical support, with the total sample 5 percent, but 16 percent of Led Zeppelin fans considered themselves radical.

MEAN AGE

A study of the age of supporters can be revealing. The mean age of the total sample was 19.6 years, with Bob Dylan fans being the oldest at 20.4 years. They were followed by the Crosby, Stills, Nash and Young crowd and the Who fans at 20.0 years. The groups that had the youngest fans were Deep Purple (18.5), Alice Cooper (18.7), and Pink Floyd and the Carpenters (18.8 years).

REACTIONS TO WORDS AND PHRASES AND PEOPLE

College students (6.9 sample response on a scale of 1 to 10). Chicago and Who fans related most positively to these words for they rated them 7.7. Alice Cooper fans rated lowest at 6.0.

Indians (6.6 sample mean score on a scale of 1 to 10). Pink Floyd ranked highest at 7.4, followed by Chicago at 7.0, and Alice Cooper at 7.0. The Carpenters and Deep Purple people scored the lowest with a neutral 5.0.

Blacks (6.3 sample score on a scale of 1 to 10). Allman Brothers Band fans seem to have had the least racist tendencies as they rated this word 7.3. Alice Cooper fans finished second at 7.0. The Carpenters' fans had the least positive response at a neutral 4.7.

Jews (6.0 sample score on a scale of 1 to 10). Chicago had the highest positive response at 8.0. Crosby, Stills, Nash, and Young fans followed at 7.4. Carpenter fans had the lowest at a neutral 4.0 mean score.

Police (5.2 sample ranking on a scale of 1 to 10). Alice Cooper people related most positively ranking this law-and-order symbol higher than any other group at 8.5. Elton John fans followed with a 6.8 score. Allman Brothers fans had the most negative reaction to the word at 3.9.

Richard Nixon (3.8 sample score on a scale of 1 to 10). The group whose fans were most positive towards the name of the then president was the Carpenters at 4.3. Elton John fans followed at 4.2 and Alice Cooper people at 4.0. Deep Purple fans were most repulsed by the word *Nixon*, they gave it 1.0 mean score. Other scores were Tull (1.6), Allmans (1.7), Carly-Joni-Carole (1.8), and Dylan and CSNY, 2.0.

Ted Kennedy (5.9 sample score on a scale of 1 to 10). Alice Cooper fans gave the most positive ranking at 7.5. CSNY followed at 6.8. The Carpenters had the most negative reaction at 3.3.

Mick Jagger (5.9 sample score on a scale of 1 to 10). Rolling Stone fans had the most positive response at 8.8. Tull fans followed with the next most positive reaction at 8.1. Cat Stevens' fans had the lowest score at 4.4. The next lowest score came from the fans of the female singers at 4.5.

Gloria Steinem (5.2 sample response on a scale of 1 to 10). Jethro Tull fans reacted most positively at 6.4. Fans of the macho-sexist Stones registered at 6.2. Deep Purple people the most negative ranking at 3.5, and Alice Cooper and Who fans were the next lowest scores at 4.0. Fans of the female singers were neutral.

Angela Davis (sample rated at 4.6 on a scale of 1 to 10). Dylan fans and CSNY people rated their reactions at 5.4. Allmans fans closely followed at 5.3. Yes fans responded with 5.2, and Stones fans gave their reaction a 5.1. Elton John fans were most turned off at 2.8. Cooper fans followed at 3.0. Thus Alice Cooper fans and Elton John people responded more positively to *Richard Nixon* than to *Angela Davis!*

Legalized marijuana (7.1 sample score on a scale of 1 to 10). Allman Brothers Band followers responded positively at 9.6. Yes people followed at 9.4. Cat Stevens' fans (6.2), Elton John people (6.6), and Carpenter followers (6.7) were the least positive toward legalizing marijuana.

Legalized drinking for eighteen-year-olds in Indiana (8.4 sample rating on a scale of 1 to 10). Yes and Pink Floyd people gave this symbol a 9.4. The Allman Brothers Band fans followed at 9.3. Elton John and Bob Dylan followers gave the issue a 7.6 to rank lowest in positive feelings.

Protestants (6.1 mean score for sample on a scale of 1 to 10). Carpenter fans had a positive response of 8.3; Alice Cooper people were the next most positive as they registered 7.5. Elton John (7.2) and Chicago (7.1) fans followed. Tull, Yes, and Carly-Joni-Carole fans were the least positive at a neutral 5.4.

Whites (6.8 sample score on a scale of 1 to 10). Chicago people were the most positive at 8.6. Carpenters followed at 8.3, and Alice Cooper fans related to the word at a 7.5 score. Pink Floyd fans were the least positive at a neutral 5.4, followed by Carly-Joni-Carole supporters at 5.8.

Legalized abortion (7.3 sample score on a scale of 1 to 10). Pink Floyd people had a positive reaction of 9.0; Deep Purple people followed with 8.5; and the Allmans and Carly-Joni-Carole fans were next at 8.2. Cat Stevens supporters were the least positive at 4.7.

Henry Kissinger (6.1 sample score on a scale of 1 to 10). Alice Cooper, Carpenters, and Who fans responded most positively at 8.0. Deep Purple fans (5.0) and Pink Floyd fans (5.2) responded least positively.

Women's Liberation (6.0 sample score on a scale of 1 to 10). CSNY people responded to these words with 6.8, followed by the Moody Blues at 6.7. The Carpenter fans responded most negatively at 4.3 followed by Deep Purple fans at 4.5.

George McGovern (5.9 sample on a scale of 1 to 10). Deep Purple fans were the most positive at 8.0. The Stones' supporters ranked second at 7.2. Carpenter fans reacted negatively at 3.7, with Elton John fans scoring at 4.3.

Amnesty for draft evaders (6.2 mean score on a score of 1 to 10). Rolling Stones fans were most positive at 8.2, followed by Deep Purple and Tull people at 7.9. Carpenter fans scored the words at 3.3. Alice Cooper people scored at 4.0, and Elton John supporters at 5.3.

POW (7.5 sample score on a scale of 1 to 10). Alice Cooper fans were the most positive to this political symbol; they responded at 9.0. Elton John fans were the next most positive at 8.8. Carpenters fans (8.3) and Chicago supporters (8.0) followed. Cat Stevens people were less positive at 6.2, as were Tull, Deep Purple, and Yes fans at 6.5.

Bob Dylan (7.0 sample score on a scale of 1 to 10). Dylan fans naturally responded to this word in the most positive fashion at 9.2. Carpenters fans were next at 9.0. (Perhaps they are not listening to Dylan's lyrics as evidenced by their conservative rankings elsewhere.) The Stones people gave *Dylan* an 8.4. The performers whose fans were least positive were Cat Stevens and Alice Cooper at 6.0.

Mao Tse-Tung (4.6 sample mean score on a scale of 1 to 10). The Moody Blues people related best to Mao at 6.2. Cat Stevens fans and the Allman crowd were next with 5.5 and 5.3, respectively. Carpenters fans were most repulsed at 3.0. Only Carpenter and Elton John fans scored *Richard Nixon* higher than *Mao*. Sixteen of the eighteen groups of fans were less positive toward the president of the United States than toward the former leader of the People's Republic of China.

George Wallace (3.8 sample score on a scale of 1 to 10). Alice Cooper fans seem to like almost anybody. They were the most positive toward *Wallace* at 6.5. Who fans were second at a neutral 4.7. Pink Floyd fans and the fans of the female singers gave the most negative response of 2.0.

Antiwar protesters (5.6 sample score on a scale of 1 to 10). Alice Cooper fans were the most positive at 7.5. Next came the Allman Brothers Band people (6.9) and the Beatles' supporters (6.8). Then followed the Stones crowd (6.5) and CSNY at 6.5. The Carpenters' fans were most repulsed by the image conveyed to them by these words and scored them 3.7. Elton John people were next in negative reactions at 4.6.

THE WATERGATE QUESTIONS

1. Do you think President Nixon had prior knowledge that the Watergate break-in was going to happen? (Mean: 64 percent)

Group	Percent of fans who responded
CSNY	85
Yes	85
Jethro Tull	79
Deep Purple	77
Bob Dylan	76
Alice Cooper	57
Moody Blues	56
Elton John	56
Pink Floyd	50
Who	43

2. Do you think President Nixon was involved in a Watergate cover-up to obstruct justice? (Mean: 88 percent)

Carpenters	100
Allman Brothers	100
Jethro Tull	100
CSNY	95
Bob Dylan	95
Cat Stevens	82
Deep Purple	77
Alice Cooper	69

3. Do you think President Nixon has told the American people
   the truth about Watergate and other related incidents?
   (Mean: 12 percent)

Alice Cooper	33
Pink Floyd	25
Cat Stevens	18
Carpenters	17
Rolling Stones	2
Allman Brothers, Yes, Who, Jethro Tull, Bob Dylan	0

4. Do you think President Nixon should be impeached if it could
   be proven that he had prior knowledge that the Watergate
   break-in was going to happen? (Mean: 64 percent)

Allman Brothers	84
Who	83
Bob Dylan	81
Cat Stevens	73
Elton John	54
Alice Cooper	40
Carpenters	0

5. Do you think President Nixon should be impeached if it could
   be proven that he was involved in Watergate cover-up to
   obstruct justice? (Mean: 57 percent)

Allman Brothers	95
Who	83
Bob Dylan	76
Cat Stevens	73
Yes	70
Deep Purple	70
Alice Cooper	33
Chicago	32
Elton John	29
Carpenters	0

From the responses to the Watergate questions, it seemed that Richard Nixon was in trouble. The sample was drawn from students in the heartland, Ball State University in Muncie, Indiana, and Indiana University. All the Carpenter fans believed Nixon was involved in a cover-up to obstruct justice, yet not one Carpenter fan would impeach him if it could be proven that he had prior knowledge about Watergate or if it could be proven that he had obstructed justice. In contrast, The Allman Brothers Band fans were "on to Nixon" and were ready to "nail him to the wall." The same is true for Bob Dylan and Who fans.

In another revealing question, the students were asked whom, if anyone, they supported for president in 1972 election, Nixon or McGovern? Alice Cooper fans gave Nixon the greatest support with 86 percent. Carpenter fans supported Nixon in 1972 with 80 percent of their numbers backing the president. Elton John fans followed (74 percent), and then came Chicago fans (63 percent). The sample backing for Nixon over McGovern in 1972 was 43 percent. The Allman Brothers Band crowd supported McGovern at 94 percent. Then followed Yes (76 percent), Jethro Tull (75 percent), Led Zeppelin (74 percent), and Pink Floyd (72 percent). The sample mean support for McGovern was 57 percent.

THE BEHAVIOR QUESTIONS

1. Have you ever smoked marijuana? (Sample mean: 67 percent)

One hundred percent of Allman Brothers Band supporters had used marijuana. Jethro Tull fans followed with 95 percent trying marijuana, and Yes fans, 95 percent. The Led Zeppelin crowd followed with 84 percent and then came Dylan fans and Stones people at 82 percent. Chicago fans had the lowest score on marijuana use at 10 percent. The Carpenters followed at 33 percent, and then came Cat Stevens's fans at 36 percent, Alice Cooper fans (46 percent) and Elton John people (46 percent).

2. Do you smoke marijuana at least once a month? (Sample mean: 35 percent)

Allman Brothers Band supporters led with 79 percent, followed by fans of Yes, 75 percent, Jethro Tull, 60 percent, Led Zeppelin, 53 percent, Bob Dylan, 50 percent, and Rolling Stones, 47 percent. Three groups had no supporters who smoked marijuana at least once a week: Carpenters, Chicago, and the Who. Elton John fans were the next lowest with only 4 percent using grass at least once a week.

3. Do you currently use any other illegal drugs? (Sample mean: 20 percent)

Allman Brothers Band fans again led with 53 percent claiming to use some type of illegal drug other than marijuana. Led Zeppelin followed (47 percent) and then came Stones fans (47 percent), Pink Floyd people (44 percent) and Yes fans (40 percent). It was interesting to note that 11 percent of the Stones crowd used cocaine. Four groups' fans had no other illegal drug use: Chicago, Carpenters, Alice Cooper, and Elton John.

4. How many hours per week do you listen to rock music? (Sample mean: 24.9 hours)

Deep Purple fans listened to rock music the most at 32.5 hours per week. Then came fans of Yes (32.2 hours), Stones (29.9), Carly-Joni-Carole (29.4), Alice Cooper (28.4), and Bob Dylan (26.9). On the other end of the scale, Carpenter fans listened to rock music the least amount of time, 10.0 hours per week. Pink Floyd and the Moody Blues fans listened 18.7 hours per week. Then came Beatles supporters (19.9), Elton John (20.2), and Led Zeppelin (20.2).

SUMMARY

After looking at the data from the rock survey, one can see that knowing a person's favorite group can in some situations help predict his or her political attitudes, and, in some cases, behavior. While some groups attract a certain type of fan, other groups are liked by a wide range of political composites. Forty-three tables were constructed from the surveys. Fans of performers were rated from most liberal to most conservative on thirty-three of the tables. The groups that most significantly deviated from the mean score in either direction and thus were the most consistently predictive across the board were: Carpenters (thirty-six significant appearances in the tables), Alice Cooper (thirty-two significant appearances), Elton John (twenty-nine significant appearances), Allman Brothers Band (twenty-seven appearances), Deep Purple (twenty-five appearances) and Pink Floyd (twenty-four appearances). The groups that were least consistently predictive across the board were: Moody Blues (only eight significant appearances), Beatles (nine appearances), Crosby, Stills, Nash, and Young and Led Zeppelin (fourteen each).

When one ranks each group on thirty-three liberal to conservative scales that were constructed on certain items, one is in a position to develop a liberal-radical table (see figure 4.1).

Fig. 4.1
Liberal-radical rankings.*

	Rank		Summed Score	
	33	20	33	20
Liberal Fans	Scales	Scales	Scales	Scales
Allman Brothers Band	1	(1)	169	96
Yes	2	(5)	193	135
Rolling Stones	3	(3)	206	114
Crosby, Stills, Nash, and Young	4	(4)	217	118
Jethro Tull	5	(2)	235	113
Bob Dylan	6	(6)	244	145
Middle-of-the-Road Fans				
Pink Floyd	7	(9)	252	172
Deep Purple	8	(7)	255	158
Led Zeppelin	9	(8)	292	167
Beatles	10	(10)	304	180
Carly-Joni-Carole	11	(11)	315	185
Chicago	12	(13)	339	212
Moody Blues	13	(14)	341	216
Who	14	(15)	349	226
Cat Stevens	14	(12)	349	203
Conservative Fans				
Alice Cooper	16	(16)	388	250
Elton John	17	(17)	453	286
Carpenters	18	(18)	481	314

*Groups rated from most liberal-radical to most conservative. Scores are the summation of thirty-three rankings on thirty-three liberal-conservative scales developed from the responses.

Allman Brothers fans were clearly the most consistently liberal-radical group. The findings about the Yes supporters were surprising because their fans rated higher on the liberal-radical scale than the older, more political groups' fans such as Rolling Stones, CSNY, and Bob Dylan. The fans of the Beatles, Moody Blues, Chicago, Who, Cat Stevens, and Carly-Joni-Carole were drawn from many different political persuasions, which made these groups not very predictive on liberal-conservative political questions; they fell into a middle-of-the-road pattern. The supporters of Alice Cooper, Elton John, and the Carpenters were consistently conservative. This finding about Alice Cooper fans is remarkable when one considers Cooper's stage show and all its implications for crowd behavior.[28] One might think that Cooper's style of stage theatrics would attract a more liberal fan, but in this research this was not the case. Alice Cooper fans were conservative across the board, though not to the extreme that Elton John or Carpenter fans were.

It is unfortunate that this study did not get enough respondents for other groups to show the composite political belief of fans of Grateful Dead, Byrds, Mothers of Invention, Jefferson Airplane, Eagles, Arlo Guthrie, Van Morrison, Rod Stewart, James Taylor, or Leon Russell. Out of 345 respondents these artists had only one or two fans each. It is equally unfortunate that the total sample was only about 1 percent black. It would have been interesting to see the responses of the fans of James Brown, Stevie Wonder, Curtis Mayfield, Isaac Hayes, Aretha Franklin, War, or the Jackson Five.

The Second Study

In 1980 my first study was duplicated at Fairfield University by Michael DiDonato and Chris Pfirrman in an effort to see if there was a relationship between a person's favorite rock group and his or her particular politics. After questioning 350 college students on their favorite rock stars and political attitudes, DiDonato and Pfirrman found that Bruce Springsteen had the most first-place votes for favorite rock star or group with thirty-two. The Beatles finished second with twenty-eight fans.

Using the data gathered by DiDonato and Pfirrman, one can make judgments about the political attitudes of various fans of specific rock groups in the 1980s. Ten fans of the Rolling Stones, when asked to rank twenty-six terms, gave the highest ranking to *premarital sex*. Stones' fans gave the term a 1.4 out of a possible 2.0 average score. On a scale that ranged from positive 2 to 0 to negative 2, the average response for *parents* by Stones' fans was positive 1.2. The term to which Stones' fans gave the most negative response was *Ronald Reagan* at negative .8.

Punk rock and new wave fans on the other hand gave their most positive response to the word *blacks* at 1.83 out of a possible 2.00. They gave *Ronald Reagan* a negative .83 score, but the term that most repulsed them was *disco*, which received a perfect negative 2.0 score.

Fans of female singers, such as Linda Ronstadt, Carly Simon, Joni Mitchell, and Bonnie Raitt, gave their highest positive responses to *parents*, *religion*, *marriage*, and *children*, each receiving a positive 1.44 score out of a possible 2.00 average score. These fans gave *nuclear power plants* a score of negative 1.22.

Sixteen of the Billy Joel fans gave *children* a perfect positive 2.00 score and *marriage* a positive 1.94 out of a possible 2.00. *Parents* also received high marks from Billy Joel fans at an average score of positive 1.87. Bruce Springsteen fans gave their top three average scores to *parents*, *marriage*, and *children*, each of which scored a positive 1.63 out of a possible 2.00.

Donna Summer fans gave their highest scores to *disco* and *parents*, both terms receiving a positive 2.00 average score. But Grateful Dead fans gave their highest score to *marijuana* with a score of 1.58. Grateful Dead fans most hated the term *disco* with a score of negative 1.48. Jackson Browne fans gave their highest marks to *children* with a positive 2.00 average score while *marriage* followed with an average score of positive 1.93.

In terms of behavioral characteristics of various groups' fans, 90 percent of the Stones' fans interviewed drank alcoholic beverages and 60 percent smoked marijuana. Moreover, 50 percent used some other drugs, particularly cocaine. There were no female fans in the survey who listed the Rolling Stones as their top group. In regard to fans of punk rock and new wave, 83 percent drank alcoholic beverages and 67 percent smoked marijuana. Yet only 22 percent of the fans of female singers smoked marijuana. Of the people who listed various female singers as their top favorites, only 11 percent were males.

Of Beatles fans, 33 percent smoked marijuana and only 7 percent used some other form of drugs. A majority or 60 percent of the Beatles' fans were women. Billy Joel fans were 68 percent female, and only one in four of Joel's fans smoked marijuana. No Billy Joel fan used any other drugs. Of Bruce Springsteen's fans, 52 percent had smoked marijuana, but no fan out of 30 used any other drugs.

Donna Summer fans were 80 percent female; 40 percent smoked marijuana and 20 percent used some other form of illegal drugs. Yet 100 percent of Grateful Dead fans surveyed here had used marijuana, while 75 percent used other drugs. Seventy-five percent of Jackson Browne's fans were female; only 33 percent had smoked marijuana and only 16 percent had used other drugs.

From the data of the second study, it appears that rock music in the 1980s is even less political than it was in the mid-1970s, the period of the first study. The rock fans at Fairfield University related positively to children, parents, religion, and marriage. The rock fan had hardly been radicalized by the sounds of middle-of-the-road artists like Billy Joel, Donna Summer, Jackson Browne, or the female singers. On political questions, only the fans of the Rolling Stones and those of punk rock/new wave bands exhibited the slightest of political tendencies. These tendencies were essentially anti-Reagan in nature.

As far as drug usage goes, only the fans of the Grateful Dead and Rolling Stones exhibited unusually high correlations with smoking marijuana and using cocaine. The politics of rock music in the 1980s, in terms of "you are what you listen to," is virtually dead except that generated by the Grateful Dead and punk rock/new wave groups. However, this turn of events is not expected to continue since rock music should reflect what goes on in society. Rock music in the 1980s might begin to reflect some new political themes in response to Ronald Reagan's policies.

5/ Bob Dylan

IN UNDERTAKING A STUDY OF the philosophical and political positions of Bob Dylan, poet, songwriter, and musician, it becomes necessary to remember that Dylan's songs are not meant to be great. Nor is Dylan meant to be great, according to him. Dylan said, "I don't think anything I touch is destined for greatness. Genius is a terrible word, a word they think will make me like them. A genius is a very insulting thing to say. Even Einstein wasn't a genius. He was a foreign mathematician who could have stolen cars."[1] However, Dylan has spawned a generation of poets and songwriters and has become a spokesman and symbol of the youth cult, much to his apparent disliking. Dylan has often stated that the many writers and college students all over America who were "hung up" on his words were missing the whole point. Dylan says that he doesn't want anybody to be hung up, especially not over him or anything he does.

With this in mind, and after dismissing the Dylan syndrome, "Dylan as God," it is much easier to proceed with the views of Bob Dylan. To arrive at the "Dylan philosophy" by analyzing the lyrics of his many songs becomes a worthwhile project. However, one is on very risky ground in interpreting song lyrics or poems by Dylan so as to arrive at his philosophy, since a poem or song lyric is not an easily analyzed entity. Song lyrics and poems are not "true" or "false" statements, according to some philosophers, and are open to a wide range of interpretations. To mold a philosophical statement out of a song or poem becomes a subjective enterprise for the researcher.

EXISTENTIALIST BOB DYLAN?

Dylan holds a certain attitude toward life, death, and the aftermath. Dylan accepts chaos, but he is not sure whether or not it accepts him.[2] He accepts everything that is around him because it is here, because it is real, and because it exists. He feels that he can't just turn himself off to his experiences, because if he tries to fight what is real and exists, he will only end up going insane faster than he normally would. "Try to deal with the existential reality" is Dylan's view.

With his subjective "truth," his situational ethics, his discussion and relation with the "other," his acceptance of his "facticities" and his approach to the problem of knowing quality, Dylan must qualify as a type of existentialist. When Dylan states, "God, I'm glad I'm not me," isn't he denying the existence of a transcendent ego as Sartre has already done? That is, the "I" is not the final stopping point in the phenomenological reduction of the mind as some suggest, but rather consciousness is the irreducible state. Dylan is glad that he is not "himself" or "me" as others have defined him, and he is glad that the product called his "ego" is not actually him, but rather some kind of construction or fabrication made by others so that they can define him. Dylan feels that you are anything that you say you are and that no one can define what it means to be you or falsely construct your ego. If you believe that you are nothing and say you are small, then to Dylan, you are nothing and are small.

Death is another subject in the Dylan philosophy that plays a central focal point; death seems to be the end. Dylan once said (in relation to the existential situation), "I would not like to be Bach, Mozart, Tolstoy, Joe Hill, Gertrude Stein, or James Dean. They are all dead."[3] Though he admits that he really doesn't understand too well what is happening on this earth, he does know that we are all going to die some day and that no one's death has ever stopped the world. Each of us has a decision to make, according to Dylan, as to how seriously we should take ourselves in the face of the absurd situation. He says, "I'm saying that you're going to die, and you're gonna go off the earth, you're gonna be dead. Man, it could be, you know, twenty years, it could be tomorrow, any time, so am I. I mean, we're just gonna be gone. The world's going to go on without us. All right now, you do your job in the face of that and how seriously you take yourself, you decide for yourself. Okay, now I'll decide for myself."[4]

Dylan does have a fear of decay. He feels that decay is "something that has stopped living, but hasn't died yet." He once said, "Decay turns me off. I'll die first before I decay!"[5]

In the 1960s Dylan did not believe in the Christian concept of God. He did not feel that he was religious, if you define religion as going to church every Sunday or bowing down to some idol. He claimed that he didn't believe in anything, and why should he? He didn't see anything to believe in.[6] He didn't feel that this position was cynical because he could not accept anything that anybody offered him to believe in. He was not going to believe in or put all his trust and faith in something because, as he once said, "Nothing is sacred, man!" Though many reporters, reviewers, and students of Dylan draw similarities between things that Dylan said in his songs and the Bible, Dylan claimed to have never read the Bible, but he did admit to having glanced through it.

DESOLATION ROW

No sooner had Bob Dylan taken us from home in "Just Like Tom Thumb's Blues," than he brought us all back home again in "Desolation Row." The question left for us to deal with is, Where did Dylan bring us home to? Where is "Desolation Row?"

Any time one tries to explain or interpret Dylan's multiple-image, lyrical poetry, one is on shaky ground, especially when one tries to come to terms with a song that is Dylan at perhaps his most mystical obscure moments. If you try to explain a Dylan song, you often limit its possibilities.

"Desolation Row," the delightful ten stanza song poem that Dylan chose to end his album *Highway 61 Revisited*, is no doubt the place that lies at the end of "Highway 61." A narrow view of "Desolation Row" might see the place as the living quarters of the carnival-circus crowd that Dylan is so fond of and often uses specifically in his image weaving. But "Desolation Row" more accurately reflects the depression felt in relationships of people in the cities. Dylan is describing everyday life. We are all in such absurd situations as those in "Desolation Row."

In the last lines of "Just Like Tom Thumb's Blues" (the song that precedes "Desolation Row"), Dylan announces that he's going to New York City. (Perhaps "Desolation Row" is the Village in New York City.) "Desolation Row" is anywhere that reflects those absurd situations in life that Dylan tells us about through the various characters that he knows and we know.

Absurd situations are our reality, situations like businessmen selling postcards of a hanging and a beauty parlor filled with sailors. A blind commissioner is coming down the road pawing the tightrope walker with one hand and masturbating with the other. Cinderella, the all-American prostitute, is forced to deal with our all-American lady-killer, Romeo, who winds up being taken away from his horny desires.

In stanza three, darkness begins to cover "Desolation Row" as the fortune-teller takes the things inside. All seem to be making love, except for people like Cain and Abel or physical freaks like the hunchback or the liberal who is dressing up to go to "Desolation Row" to see the freak show and maybe offer a little help. Ophelia is totally messed up in the mind and wishes it was all over. Her rejection and depression make death quite appealing to her. Einstein, who let his great career get away, is now into snorting drain pipes. Doctor Filth has all the medical and scientific power over us as we go to him for advice, but his approach along with the local nurse is a sad death trip for his sexless patients.

We sent a letter to Bob Dylan asking him if he could tell us what all of our friends were doing on "Desolation Row." He sent back his reply in the form of the song after he had rearranged all their faces and given them all new names. He told us about our friends and freaks such as the phantom of the opera and the sexually hung-up Cassanova, who is being treated for a lack of self-confidence.

Stanza eight indicates the fascism and repression that is all around us as we try to live through another day on "Desolation Row." Dylan is at his best here in a continuation of his criticism of the repressive state of politics which he painted for us in "It's Alright Ma (I'm only Bleeding)" from the *Bringing It All Back Home* album.

Dylan tells us that confusion and fighting are raging as the ship is going down, with Pound and Eliot fighting. With the storm raging in the city, Bob Dylan doesn't mind answering more questions about our friends in "Desolation Row," but we had better mail all of our inquiries from the place of desolation or he won't answer us. In effect Dylan is telling us to quit watching the freak show from our comfortable chair in suburbia and get on "down home" to where he and our freaky friends are residing in "Desolation Row."

THE POLITICS OF BOB DYLAN

Bob Dylan, perhaps more than any other contemporary artist, is responsible for the phenomenon of "political rock." Dylan liberated the lyrics and established the basic parameters for political rock music early in his career. A content analysis of most rock lyrics over the past twenty years reveals very little of political import. But the few rock songs that one might classify as political in nature usually draw from the early Dylan style.

Of course, the irony of all this is the fact that Dylan has never been political. Politics, political stands, commitment, mass movements have all been foreign to Dylan. When Dylan made the switch from pure folk to rock and dropped most of his political themes, his political fans and his pure folk fans cried that Dylan was selling out. But the question remains, How could Dylan sell out when he never was committed in the first place?

To be sure, Dylan's early songs contained some of the most powerful political messages ever recorded. "Masters of War," "With God on Our Side," "Chimes of Freedom," "The Times They Are a'Changin'," "Blowin' in the Wind," "Subterranean Homesick Blues," and "Only a Pawn in Their Game," show Dylan taking overt political stands in his folk poetry. Yet, it is very difficult to characterize Dylan's political ideology from his early folk songs. Dylan's messages are not clear and obvious. Somehow, though, we all knew when Dylan was being political, even if we couldn't figure out exactly what he was saying.

Dylan sang the songs of the early 1960s that protested racism, poverty, inhumanity, and war. He was the expert in witty, passionate discontent, and his poetry of protest carried a subdued, rational, moral outrage. Dylan's early connection with the "movement" was singing the songs that had never been sung before, and he captured the essence of the movement's positions in his poetry. Dylan was more of a poet and artist than a committed folksinger of protest songs, but many people viewed him only as the movement minstrel. As it turned out, Dylan would transcend such narrow limitations on his possibilities.

Jon Landau was one of the first to recognize that Dylan was acting as religious mystic and never really entered the political realm. Landau said, "He [Dylan] was simply acting out a religious allegory on the political landscape of contemporary America. His primary concerns were on the face of it moral, and moral in a religious Jewish, Christian sense."[7]

At first Dylan seemed sincere about his commitment to social protest, implied in songs like "Blowin' in the Wind." In Anthony Scaduto's definitive biography of the artist, Dylan responds to a question about his relationship to his protest songs: "The idea came to me that you were betrayed by your silence. That all of us in America who didn't speak out were betrayed by our silence. Betrayed by the silence of the people in power. They refuse to look at what is happening. And the others, they ride the subways and read the *Times*, but they don't understand. They don't know. They don't even care, that's the worst of it."[8] Dylan seemed to have forgotten his message in the late 1960s and early 1970s. To many of his followers, Dylan was betrayed by his own silence in relation to the Indochina war and America's involvement in it.

How committed was Bob Dylan to the social protest themes in his songs? The answer to this question remains a mystery. Some of Dylan's friends said Dylan was actually wrapped up in the "movement," while others feel that he was just making the scene, as usual. When asked by Joan Baez what he was thinking when he wrote all those classic songs, Dylan replied, "Hey, news can sell, right? You know me. I knew people would buy that kind of shit, right? I never was into that stuff."⁹ But given Dylan's capacity for putting people on and hiding his true feelings, how does one evaluate his comments to Baez? Can someone who wrote "With God on Our Side" not believe in that so-called "shit"? It seems unlikely that the writer of "The Times They Are a'Changin' " did not at one time sincerely believe in the song's message.

But later, Dylan told folk-rock politico Phil Ochs, "The stuff you're writing is bullshit, because politics is bullshit. It's all unreal. The only thing that's real is inside you."¹⁰ Thus Dylan evidently was the first political rocker to issue that famous statement about music and politics, though Stephen Stills would later make the same kind of statement. Dylan was also turned off to what he perceived as the absurdity of the political world. He said: "All I can say is politics is not my thing at all. I can't see myself on a platform talking about how to help people. Because I would get myself killed if I really tried to help anybody. I mean if somebody really had something to say to help somebody out, just bluntly say the truth, well obviously they're gonna be done away with. They're gonna be killed."¹¹

Dylan was hesitant to join movements. He did not think it was pointless to dedicate oneself to peace and racial equality; it was pointless to dedicate oneself to a "cause."¹² Movement leaders to Dylan could be just as full of "bullshit" as political leaders. When talking about the civil rights movement, Dylan once said, "But when you get beneath it, like anything, you find there's bullshit tied up in it."¹³ This Dylan attitude toward movements and their leaders may help in examining Dylan's reluctance to become part of the Vietnam antiwar movement in action or in song.

Despite the fact that Dylan could be considered only part of the "movement" via his songs for a few short years, some critics have given Dylan credit in setting the spiritual guidance for protest in the 1960s. Theodore Roszak, who wrote *The Making of a Counter Culture*, said about Dylan: "All at once Dylan is somewhere beneath the rationalizing cerebrum of social discourse, probing the nightmare deeps, trying to get at the tangled roots of conduct and opinion. At this point, the project which beats of the early fifties had taken up the task of remodeling themselves, their way of life, their perceptions and sensitivities, rapidly takes precedence over the public task of changing institutions or policies."[14] Critic Scott Sullivan, overwhelmed by the Dylan mystique, wrote, "The movement of the youth in America against imperialist war, racism, and all forms of exploitation (including that of the earth) has already begun, and we must give credit where credit is due to Bob Dylan's genius (from Latin genius—guardian spirit) for getting us started on our way."[15]

Dylan faded from the scene for a while after his motorcycle accident, but this seclusion only added to the Dylan myth. When he re-emerged, he came back as a religious mystic in *John Wesley Harding*. Then Dylan became the respected country-and-western star in *Nashville Skyline*. Next came Dylan as a faded, rock-culture version of Frank Sinatra in *Self Portrait*. This came during a time of intense political protest over the war and other injustices committed by the U.S. government, but Dylan remained silent. At the time when most "movement" people needed their minstrel Bob Dylan to speak most, all he said was "Lay Lady Lay" and "Take Me as I Am."

Dylan ushered in the 1970s with *New Morning*, and there was hope that he was coming around again musically and in terms of a stand against social injustice. Musically the album scored well, but politically Dylan only expounded his love of the land and "back to nature" values.

In 1971 Bob Dylan became politicized again. In August he performed at the George Harrison-Ravi Shankar concert for Bangladesh. Dylan had come out this time to raise money for Bangladesh refugees. Dylan's myth was celebrated in old memories like "Blowin' in the Wind," "A Hard Rain's a-Gonna Fall," "Mr. Tambourine Man," "Just Like a Woman," and "It Takes a Lot to Laugh/It Takes a Train to Cry."

Dylan continued his politicization in late 1971 and early 1972 with his ballad "George Jackson."[16] Dylan was now singing about a black political prisoner. This excited his old political fans, but some critics could not figure out why he would come out with such a song at that particular time. There had been other political happenings for Dylan to cover in song, such as the 1968 Democratic national convention and police riot, the assassinations of Robert Kennedy and Martin Luther King, Jr., the Indochina war, the invasion of Cambodia, the May Day arrests. Why did he pick the murder of George Jackson? Obviously, he wasn't trying to create a million-selling single, since many stations refused to play it because of the "philosophy" of the song or because of Dylan's use of the word shit.[17] Perhaps he was just sending out signals to his social critics and his fans that he was still politically involved. And Dylan, the rumor had it, was not that popular among some Black Panther leaders because he had refused to do a Panther benefit. Dylan allegedly told them, "I can't help you as long as the Panthers are against Israel,"[18] which was a response to being called a "Zionist pig."[19]

Dylan remained silent during the 1972 presidential election, and in 1973 he entered his cowboy rock period with *Pat Garrett and Billy the Kid*, a movie directed by Sam Peckinpah. But in 1974 Bob Dylan returned to live performance by touring the nation. Nineteen seventy-four was not only the year of Richard Nixon's impending impeachment, it was also the year of Bob Dylan in the rock world. Dylan joined forces with the Band and recorded a new album, *Planet Waves*, but the main event, of course, was the Bob Dylan tour.

Dylan was the consummate rock and roll star, up there on stage swinging his electric guitar around and shuffling his feet. He even turned the volume way up for the new style of rock listening. Something was happening and Mr. Jones did not know what it was when he saw 18,000 people dance and boogie to "Blowin' in the Wind."

The live Dylan Band concert album captured the excitement. When Dylan sang "Like a Rolling Stone," people rose to their feet, sang along, clapped, danced, shouted, listened, boogied, and smiled. It captured that late-1960s spirit of community and commitment that had been missing in rock culture. But one also must recognize that of those people who voted within this Dylan audience in 1972, Nixon probably carried the majority. No matter, the concert was a return to 1960s commitment, rock, politics, and good times. The concert was also a rebirth for Dylan.

Dylan, the rock capitalists' capitalist, scored millions of dollars during this new period of inflation rock. Ticket prices were outrageous, and many people said, "I saw the Dead play for four hours and it was free." Rumors had Dylan giving a large hunk of his intake, around $4 million to Israel for their struggle with the Arabs, but there were no confirmations. "Who cares what Dylan does with his money as long as he plays for us," most people reacted. Later, it was learned that Dylan lost around $78,000 in the celebrity oil-well drilling scheme. Dylan had gotten burned along with many other celebrities who had hoped to strike it richer. Dylan had indeed come a long way from singing songs about rural poverty. The public finally saw what many had privately feared, economically and politically Dylan was a little to the left of Jack Benny and Liza Minnelli.

Bob Dylan entered the 1980s as largely irrelevant to many young people. He had put together the "born-again Christian" rock album called *Slow Train Coming* and the 1980 album *Saved*. Dylan had alienated most of his earlier political followers as they, too, reached middle age. Dylan's message was simply "love Jesus and do His work." In the 1980s context, faced with the growing loss of his rock fans, perhaps this was really Dylan at his most political, i.e., a servant of the Lord. His album in 1981, *Shot of Love*, continued the "Dylan as Billy Graham" theme, but in 1982 Dylan did find time to play some of the antinuclear protest concerts. The times they were a-changin' once again, it seemed.

6/ The Rolling Stones

FROM THE BEGINNING, WITH THEIR first album *The Rolling Stones* (May 1964), the Stones presented an alternative to the choirboy sound of the Beatles. The Stones sang the raunchy "I'm a King Bee" while the Beatles sang "I Wanna Hold Your Hand." Mick Jagger, Keith Richards, Brian Jones, Charlie Watts, and Bill Wyman had longer hair and appeared unkempt, while the Beatles resembled uniformed carnival dolls. The myth grew as the Stones released two more albums, but these did not sell as well as those of other British groups during the "British invasion" of 1964-65. The Stones were just another British group, although there were a small number of fanatics who recognized the Stones' blues talent as exhibited in these first three albums.

With the 1965 release of "(I Can't Get No) Satisfaction," perhaps the best rock song ever recorded, and their fourth album, *Out of Our Heads* (July 1965), the Rolling Stones established themselves as superstars, and in some circles as the greatest group in the world, even topping the Beatles.

Jagger's myth grew, and the Stones put out *December's Children* (November 1965). They continued with *Aftermath* (June

1966), which was better than anything they had previously done. Then came a minor lull with *Got Live If You Want It* (November 1966), *Between the Buttons* (January 1967), and *Flowers* (June 1967) before they attempted to out-Beatle the Beatles during the creative rock explosion of 1967 (when we were Sgt. Peppered, Jefferson Airplaned, Doored, Creamed, and Hendrixed) with *Their Satanic Majesties Request* (November 1967).

Growing musically, the Rolling Stones turned out *Beggars Banquet* (November 1968) and *Let It Bleed* (1969). Brian Jones had died, but the Stones carried on with Mick Taylor in their 1969 rock concert tour of the United States, a success in spite of the Altamont tragedies. In 1971, when many people had lost hope in many things (the Beatles had long broken up, Janis Joplin and Jimi Hendrix were dead), the Rolling Stones presented us with the sound of *Sticky Fingers* so we could all "keep the faith."

Jagger's myth had in some corners grown out of proportion, and there was little sympathy for Jagger's nonpolitical stand, his satanic folklore, and his Altamont showing. However, the Stones were alive and well, putting out rock sounds that were unparalleled. The Beatles had abdicated the throne, so the Stones were left to carry on.

THE ROLLING STONES: FIRST AND SECOND PERIODS

The Stones' recording career might be divided into four periods: the early period characterized by their first three albums *The Rolling Stones, 12 x 5,* and *The Rolling Stones Now*; the second period characterized by the group's emergence as superstars, their hit "Satisfaction," and a host of top-selling singles from 1965 to 1967; the third period characterized by the Stones' devotion to producing top albums rather than Top 40 singles and their steady growth as creative rock musicians and performers, shown in *Their Satanic Majesties Request, Beggar's Banquet, Get Your Ya-Yas Out,* and *Sticky Fingers*; and the fourth period characterized by the Stones as middle-aged rock stars.

In the early period the Stones sang the raunchy rhythm-and-blues sounds, borrowing from Chuck Berry, Muddy Waters, Bo Diddley, Willie Dixon, Howlin' Wolf, Sam Cooke, Otis Redding, Solomon Burke, and Wilson Pickett, to name a few. The Stones were more than a white British group singing the blues, like a host of other initiative bands; rather, they were blues artists sounding as good as the hallowed black saints. (Though there are many stories about how the name "Rolling Stones" came about, it is generally agreed that the Stones took their name from Muddy Waters' "Rolling Stone Blues."[1]) Jagger developed a fluid, soulful voice. The Stones stuck to the basics but their vocal and instrumental interpretations of Berry's "Carol" and "Around and Around," among others, succeeded because of the Stones' enthusiasm and devotion to the structures of rhythm and blues.

Their first album contained songs written by black blues artists, with Jagger and Richards contributing only "Tell Me," "Little by Little" (written by Nanker Phelge, a pen name for Jagger/Richards songs for which they did not want to take credit), and "Now I've Got a Witness." Relative to other Rolling Stones albums, the first release was a weak album with only "Tell Me," "Not Fade Away" (their first U.S. hit), "Carol" (later performed better on their live albums), and "I'm a King Bee" being of any lasting significance.

The second release showed the Stones' potential as they outdid Chuck Berry and created some classic rhythm and blues songs of their own. *12 x 5* clearly showed the Stones as musical perfectionists and implied that here was a vast reservoir of untapped creative rock genius. Jagger sang "Time Is on My Side" and "It's All Over Now" with complete authority and confidence in his vocal style. The Stones almost matched the legendary Drifters with a rendition of "Under the Boardwalk," and they even jammed Chicago Marshall-Chess style on "2120 South Michigan Avenue." But the real surprise of the second album was the Stones' newfound writing ability. Jagger and Richards combined for "Empty Heart," "Congratulations," and "Grown Up Wrong." Though few people in the United States were Stones fans then, Jagger was beginning to gather a cult that proclaimed him the best lead singer in rock.

The third album, *The Rolling Stones Now,* is one of my favorite Stones albums. Though there was no conscious attempt to create a unified album, this string of down-home rhythm-and-blues numbers hangs together more closely than perhaps other works. No longer were they just white imitators of black blues artists: in this album the Stones developed their own voice. They were now as much a part of the rhythm-and-blues tradition as Chuck Berry or Bo Diddley, and one could utter all three names in the same sentence without feeling guilty.

Mick Jagger captured the essence of the album when he sang "Down Home Girl." Thus the Stones' first period came to an end. They were commercial failures in the United States, although a small group of fans recognized the Stones for their blues musicianship and Jagger for his vocal impact.

The second period started with the Stones' release of "Satisfaction" and saw the group become rock artists as opposed to rhythm-and-blues artists. The second period also saw the Stones reap the ultimate compliment for a blues artist; their songs were recorded by such soul stars as Otis Redding. In the second period the Stones emerged as a commercial success, with a string of hits along the "Satisfaction" line.

Out of Our Heads kicked off the second period and it included "Satisfaction."[2] The rest of *Out of Our Heads* was not memorable, except for the songs in which Jagger started doing parodies on himself; "I'm All Right," "Play with Fire," and "The Spider and the Fly," where Jagger pokes fun at his reputation for being an exploiter of women.

Then came *December's Children.* The Stones' follow-up to "Satisfaction" was in the depression/no-satisfaction vein, called "Get Off My Cloud." Again the Stones did a Chuck Berry song "Talkin' About You," but the real gems of the album were the Jagger/Richards compositions, "As Tears Go By," "I'm Free," "Gotta Get Away," "The Singer Not the Song," and "Blue Turns to Grey," all ballads that gave relief from the harsh sounds of the screaming "She Said Yeah."

The Stones then put out *Big Hits,* which contained all their Top 40 singles, and the album, *Aftermath,* by far the Stones best effort. For the first time all the songs were written by Jagger and Richards. *Aftermath* also kicked off the start of a long string of Jagger-as-sex-exploiter songs with "Stupid Girl" and the sexist song "Under My Thumb."

The second period continued with *Got Live if You Want It.* Then came *Between the Buttons,* which showed the style of Stones-as-Dylan in many places. The Dylanesque touch showed through on "Yesterday's Papers," "Ruby Tuesday," "She Smiled Sweetly," "My Obsession," "Who's Been Sleeping Here," "Complicated," and "Something Happened to Me Yesterday." Indeed, the Stones had advanced lyrically as they showed they could write Dylan-style songs just as well as the Beatles or any other group.

Again all the songs from *Between the Buttons* were written by the Jagger/Richards team and the duo quickly became the number two writing team in rockdom behind Lennon and McCartney. The Stones closed their second period with the album titled *Flowers*. It was "deja vu" for most Stones fans since many of the songs on *Flowers* had been previously released. All the songs on the album were Jagger/Richards compositions, except for the Stones rendition of one of Motown's greatest hits, Smokey Robinson's "My Girl."

Flowers did contain some new efforts that added to the Stones myth, such as the sexist "Back Street Girl." "Mother's Little Helper" attacked the older generation's drug culture that relied on uppers and downers to face the world each day, and Jagger/Richards finished off the album in Dylanesque images created by "Ride on Baby" and "Sittin' on a Fence." *Flowers* was not a top Rolling Stones effort, but it ushered out the Stones' second period, which saw the rise of the Rolling Stones as the top rock 'n' roll band in the world.

ROCK THEATRICALITY

Whatever else one can say about Mick Jagger, one can surely claim that he was a top live performer in rockdom. The Stones, and Jagger in particular, are talented craftsmen in the art of rock theatricality. Robert Somma, in his excellent article on "rock theatricality," wrote of the Rolling Stones: "The Stones don't sell as many LP's but they do seem to outdistance the Beatles in their natural flair for the rock band role. They simply took to the stage, had more room to emote and less reserve about their personal obsessions, and brought to rock the first theatrically viable concentration of excitement....The Stones were not the least bit inhibited in their stage manners, and the excitement they generated flickered out of Jagger's faith that a rock singer could rule the world....Jagger sweated, didn't seem even to have combed his hair, maybe didn't wash, and certainly had used his lips for more than a harmonica....Jagger's pattern was to be unpredictable, to roam as he felt the urge....It wasn't so much the Stones' arrant sexuality as the appropriate candor of their stage style. They engaged the audience directly—they were intense, livid, as excitable as the teenagers....The Stones presented a dramatic persona to the audience."[3]

The Rolling Stones had added a new dimension to the role of the rock band—dynamism on stage. In fact, the Stones were often better live than on record. In describing the Stones' stage act Somma wrote, "The Stones showed that rock bands can develop in much the same way a theatre company would like to, but rock bands can do it more quickly and dynamically. For one thing, they're smaller and their material is easier to master, more instantly appealing. The Stones changed stage from a forum to a locale for the liberation of emotions."[4]

Mick Jagger on stage is a contradiction of ideas. He is a saintly, all-powerful high priest of rock. He is the original rock 'n' roll singer "out-Elvising" Presley and setting the trend for a thousand imitators. He is idolized in a Jagger-as-god syndrome. As Lester Bangs wrote, "There they were in the flesh, the Rolling Stones, ultimate personification of all our notions and fantasies and hopes for rock and roll."[5] Many fans hang on Jagger's very words as scriptures from a holy philosophy of "how to live your life as a Rolling Stone."

But Jagger is also the devil, as portrayed in his Altamont, "sympathy for the devil" myth. Jagger's rebellious life style, marijuana busts, charges of urinating in public, paternity suits, and so on, add to the myth of his satanic qualities. He is capable of leading America's good youth astray with his evil songs and actions.

Jagger is also king—his royal majesty, the king of rock stars and a top cult hero. He has become the quintessential rock celebrity.

But Jagger is also queen! He dances, prances, minces, camps, and drags himself around the stage. From under his sexy masculine voice and the "sex-ploitating" lyrics of his band's songs, Jagger on stage is a contradiction in terms. His appeal is bisexual and his appearance is feminine. Jagger is Rudolf Nureyev and

Peter Pan.[6] The Stones have a long tradition of bisexuality and camp. And there was that outrageous promotional picture of the Rolling Stones in drag for the cut "Have You Seen Your Mother, Baby." (There was Brian dolled-up like Jean Harlow; Mick looked a little like Joan Crawford with his pouting lips; Keith looked like a sexy Italian film star; and Charlie and Bill looked like old peasant women.) On the cover of *Through the Past Darkly*, Mick and Keith look especially feminine with pouting lips done in pink. On the picture in *Beggar's Banquet*, at a Rolling Stones orgy, all the lips of the members of the band are brightly painted in dark red for a very feminine effect.

On stage Jagger is a screaming queen as he entices loving sexual expressions from both sexes in the audience. Abbie Hoffman called Mick Jagger "our Myra Breckinridge."[7]

STONE POETRY AND SEXISM

The third period, which might be defined as starting with *Their Satanic Majesties Request* (November 1967) and extending to *Sticky Fingers* (May 1971), is characterized by a string of albums that show musical growth and poetic lyrics. Thematically, the Stones continued to sing about women in very sexist terms and for the first time, some people interpreted some songs from *Beggar's Banquet* as being political in nature, for example, "Sympathy for the Devil" and "Street Fighting Man."

Rock music had long been dominated by sexist lyrics and the musical scene dominated by men. The woman's liberation movement inspired a lot of talk about male supremacy in rock, and the Rolling Stones fell in line for most of the criticism. Sally Kempton, after analyzing 1960s rock lyrics, wrote, "The world of rock is the worst place in the world for a girl to find herself."[8] Judy Parker of the *Los Angeles Free Press* blamed the rock culture for keeping the sexist values of the establishment culture. She wrote, "I blame rock culture for opting for chauvinism and patriarchy in one of the only important alternative cultures that this generation has come up with."[9]

Alan Beckett's analysis of the Rolling Stones "down on women" songs incorrectly interpreted the Stones to be reflecting narcissism, but Richard Merton rightly contends that "Under My Thumb," "Stupid Girl," "Back Street Girl," or "Yesterday's

Papers" are about sexual exploitation.[10] Merton said: "[Sexual exploitation] is a permanent, structural feature of our society.... The enormous merit—and audacity—of the Stones is to have repeatedly and consistently defied what is a central taboo of the social system: mention of sexual inequality. They have done so in the most radical and unacceptable way possible: by celebrating it. The light this black beam throws on society is too bright for it. Nakedly proclaiming inequality is de facto announced. The 'unmitigated triumph' of these records is their rejection of the spurious world of monadic personal relationships. They are concerned with the oppressive matrix that is their general truth."[11]

Through their life style, the Rolling Stones did much to encourage the notion that they were "male chauvinist pigs." The Stones were heavily involved in the "groupie" social phenomenon, one of the most demeaning of all personal relationships within rockdom as it reeked of male sexism. (For the Stones part in this degrading aspect of rock, see Tom Nolan.[12]) Mick Jagger himself contributed to the "Jagger as pig" image by issuing sexist statements in many of his interviews. His most notable sexist statement probably was:

Q: Mick, what's your favorite shoe polish?
A: Here in America, I prefer Kiwi, but at home, it's Marianne's [Faithful] tongue.[13]

Jay Marks contends that the Rolling Stones are the chief exploiters of women in rock lyrics. The male double standard is mirrored in many of their pop tunes, especially in "Back Street Girl."[14] Marks said that Jagger started the trend in rock of the "stag song." Here the lead singer groans, grunts, screams, whispers, cries, snorts, growls, purrs, and sputters as in "Goin' Home." "No nuance of his [Jagger's] musical orgasm is left to the imagination," he writes. "As such his performance is likely to be better received by other males than by females, who may not be able or willing to share the self-indulgent, masturbatory illusion."[15]

The first and second period Stones songs should not be condemned as sexist. The woman's liberation movement had not yet started raising valid objections to the sexist society, and Jagger was just singing "good old rock 'n' roll" which had always been sexist. Ellen Willis has pointed out that there is a difference between the naive rock sexism that disfigured rock before, say, 1967 and the much calculated, almost ideological sexism that has flourished since: "The Stones tended to make women scapegoats for their disenchantment with the class system. Mick Jagger...brought down rich play girls with crude exhibitions of virility....Female rock fans had a great identification with the male rock stars—a relationship that all too often found us digging them while they put us down. This was not masochism but expediency. For all its limitations, rock was the best thing going, and if we had to filter out certain indignities, well we had been doing that all our lives, and there was no feminist movement to suggest that things might be different."[16]

The sexism of Mick Jagger during the third period cannot be as easily dismissed. In *Beggars Banquet*, the Stones returned to their basic rock sound, which included heavy emphasis on the blues and rock 'n' roll. It also included a return to Jagger-as-sex-exploiter on such cuts as "Stray Cat Blues," "Factory Girl," "Parachute Woman," and "Dear Doctor."

On *Let It Bleed*, the Stones continued putting out obviously sexist songs. "Honky Tonk Women" (and "Country Honk") is a classic Stones song about "naughty" girls. When the song was sung at concerts, Jagger sometimes introduced it as "for all the whores in the audience." *Let It Bleed*'s most sex-ploitation song was "Midnight Rambler."[17] Here Jagger sings tribute to a rapist!

On *Sticky Fingers*, the Stones were at their best musically, and lyrically they threw in more than their usual number of drug references. But they also continued to carry on the Jagger-as-sex-king myth. Unlike *Let It Bleed* in which the Stones took off like a jet plane in "Gimme Shelter," the Stones kicked off *Sticky Fingers* with a song that is racist and sexist, "Brown Sugar." The Stones were playing on white sexual and racial fantasies. But again the question arises, Was this type of sexism necessary from Jagger in 1971 America? The rest of the album contains relatively few sexist songs, except for Jagger/Richards "Bitch." But the Rolling Stones myth and Mick Jagger-as-exploiting-chauvinist-pig are only one aspect of the multi-dimensional

Rolling Stones musical phenomenon. The Stones are talented enough musically to survive the valid criticisms about the sexist nature of their lyrics.

THE POLITICS OF THE ROLLING STONES

While the sexism of the Rolling Stones is explicit, political aspects of the group are unrecognized. The Stones were often viewed as taking a political stand against the older generation when during the second period they produced "Satisfaction," "19th Nervous Breakdown," and "Get Off My Cloud." Some critics see the Stones as political because of their use of black rhythm and blues, suggestive lyrics, and disdain for traditions during the first and second periods. But the Stones were not making overtly political statements in the way that Bob Dylan and a few others were.

In the third period, from *Beggar's Banquet* on, the Stones picked up the label of "political band," though *Beggar's Banquet* was the only album that contained political themes, and these were vague at best: "Sympathy for the Devil," "Street Fighting Man," and "Salt of the Earth." Their limited political messages have been blown way out of proportion by many rock critics. Geoffrey Cannon writes: "The easy comparison between the Beatles and *Beggar's Banquet* is between the lyrics of 'Revolution No. 1' and 'Street Fighting Man.' The interesting comparison is between the way the songs are sung. Lennon muses his way tonelessly through his song, not seeming to mind whether or not it's heard. Jagger gives you no chance."[18]

"Revolutionary Mick" was opting for an ambiguous political position, one of realizing the necessity of the "revolution," yet not wanting to get involved. Frank McConnell called "Street Fighting Man" the "manifesto of a new social sensibility in that group."[19] The Rolling Stones had taken in some critics with their "own brand of rock and revolution."[20] Cannon, "hyped up" on "Street Fighting Man," wrote: "In 1969, a very great rock music band must speak to the people in the street. There are many different modes of relevant speech ranging from the delicate witchcraft of the Incredible String Band to the blood roar of MC 5.... The revolution has no program; its quality will be judgable in terms only of the quality of the minds of the revolutionaries. The

Acid Test has been taken. There is no retreating....*Beggar's Banquet* is crammed with apt force; with it Mick Jagger is the shaman of the emerging Western world. But the Beatles decided to stay in their hotel and feign sleep."[21]

Mick Jagger tried to keep alive the myth of "Jagger-as-street-fighting-man" during the powerful "grand return" tour of the United States in 1969. At the International Amphitheater in Chicago, the site of the 1968 Democratic convention, Jagger introduced "Street Fighting Man" to the Chicago audience (many of them veterans of the Chicago police riot during the convention) by saying, "This song is dedicated to you, Chicago-baby."[22] Jagger continued to play a pseudopolitical role throughout the song as he flashed the "peace" sign, only to appear surprised when more than half of the audience greeted his sign with boos and the more revolutionary clenched-fist "power" sign.

The Rolling Stones' masterpiece of the third period, and one of their new breed of socially aware songs, was "Sympathy for the Devil." McConnell points out that Jagger used a humanizing parodistic voice in singing about satan.[23] Musically, "Sympathy for the Devil" is one of their best works and, as Cannon writes: "Sympathy for the Devil—LET the MUSIC SPEAK. High-stepping drums, tapped delicately. Then two human cries, close to a hyena scream. Both echo, with the last, Bill Wyman starts shaking a vast maraca, sounding like a seeded gourd. The drumming is now faster with the energy of the added noises. A smaller cry. Then masculine gasps and panting, as if a microphone were held close to the face of African dancers. Now wide-spaced piano chords. Jagger begins insidiously and melodically, setting his voice up in suave contrast to the spiked music....Even at this point, seconds into a number that lasts over five minutes, there's no doubt that elemental sensations are in store."[24]

"Sympathy for the Devil" was political only in the sense that it portrayed satan as the archetypal spectator rather than the violent assassin. Satan is "everyman" who watched when Jesus Christ, the czar, and his ministers were killed; everyman who rode the tanks in Hitler's army and who watched as the Kennedys were murdered.

"Salt of the Earth" is another Stones political song in the sense that Jagger tried to pay a Marxian tribute to the working man. As

Jon Landau noted, "Jagger obviously wants to empathize with the common foot soldier, the working man, the man who is forced to throw his life away on 'back breaking work' without ever achieving satisfaction."[25] But when he looks at the masses they look strange, which points out the singer's inability to truly identify.

All three of the Rolling Stones political songs are not the kind of political statements that one associates with a movement "heavy." Landau was not taken in by the Stones-as-revolutionaries hype as he noted: " 'Salt of the Earth,' 'Street Fighting Man,' and 'Sympathy for the Devil' each are characterized lyrically by a schizoid ambiguity. The Stones are cognizant of the explosions of youthful energy that are going on all around them. They recognize the violence inherent in these struggles. They see them as movements for fundamental change and are deeply sympathetic. Yet they are too cynical to really go along themselves. After all, they are rock and roll musicians, not politicians, and London is such a 'sleepy town.' "[26]

Michael Lydon reports of the time Abbie Hoffman was in the Stones dressing room before the Chicago concert of 1969, bragging about his "movement exploits." He asked Jagger for some money for the conspiracy trials and Mick replied, "We got our own trials," and left it at that.[27] For an excellent account of Jagger as counterrevolutionary, see Richard Neville's article on Jagger's wedding.[28]

THE STONES TODAY

The Rolling Stones just keep rolling on—one gets the feeling they may never stop. The Stones were productive in the 1970s. *Exile on Main Street* was filled with rock and roll. There were a large number of religious gospel tunes—"Soul Survivor, "Just Wanna See His Face," and "Shine a Light"—and a more than usual amount of down-home raunchy sound and the usual sexist lyrics. The album, of course, was not that political since the Rolling Stones are not very political. Since they received criticism for their racist song "Brown Sugar," the Stones included "Sweet Black Angel," their only political number on *Exile*. Jagger and Richards wrote "Sweet Black Angel" as a tribute to Angela Davis, the black revolutionary.

The Stones did political numbers in *Goats Head Soup*, but "Doo Doo Doo Doo Doo (Heartbreaker)" made a new social statement. In the song, Jagger and Richards take a position against using needles when taking drugs.

The Stones sang only one political song in 1974 called "Fingerprint File," from the album *It's Only Rock'n'Roll*. Their social statements may be summed up as: have a good time, do disco (as heard on their *Some Girls* album), and treat women as sex objects. In the 1980s, the Rolling Stones remain in the rock world. While they were pioneers in rock theatricality and are innovative, they stick to the basic rock formula that has made them giants in rockdom.

7 / John Lennon

EVEN THOUGH THE EVIDENCE INDICATES that rock music in terms of its lyrical content has not been very political over the years, some performers stand out as being more political than others. Especially during the years 1967 to 1972, John Lennon ranked as the foremost politico in rock culture. Rock music tends to reflect what is going on in society rather than being an instrument of change. But if any rock songs played a key role in forming and reinforcing a new political consciousness between 1967 and 1972, Lennon's contributions with his antiwar anthem "Give Peace a Chance" would probably rank at the top of the list.

The Beatles hold an important place in an analysis of rock music and culture. They changed people's dress, hair style, social relationships, and other cultural aspects. The Beatles changed the focus of "rock 'n' roll" music to "rock." They influenced Dylan and showed him the way to go electric. If Dylan can be given credit for liberating the lyrics of rock music, then the Beatles must be given credit for liberating the music of rock. They revolutionized the rock industry with their use of technology. Though they lacked Jagger's theatricality and did not write as well as Dylan, the Beatles had an impact on rock music that far exceeded that of any other rock group or soloist. Young white Americans suddenly wanted to form their own rock bands after they heard what the Beatles were doing. American sports heroes for the first time started taking a back seat to the emerging rock and roll stars. Kids stopped asking for baseball gloves or football helmets and started asking for electric guitars. It was often a greater honor to be in the high school rock band than it was to be on the basketball team. The Beatles changed many things.

Though the Beatles were opinion leaders in establishing much of what is known as "rock culture," they were never very political in their songs. One has to stretch the meaning of some lyrics to fit them into a Beatle political statement. Fewer than 10 percent of 205 Beatle compositions studied could be said to have a political statement however slight.

The Beatles made vague political statements about nowhere people, warm guns, American machismo ethic, and pigs. They also commented on tax men, experts, war, and a man in the House of Lords. Beatles themes dealt with the inhumanity of people, and their political panacea was "All You Need Is Love." The Beatles even indulged in a little political satire in "Back in the USSR" and "Her Majesty." Lennon talked about being hassled for his beliefs in the "Ballad of John and Yoko." Only once did the Beatles feel moved to write a political song that would address the political happenings of the 1960s, and that was the Lennon-inspired "Revolution."

Of course, John Lennon was the most political Beatle. Of those songs that could in some small way be considered political, most were inspired directly by John Lennon's political world view. Until "Revolution," Lennon seemed to be content to play the part of the witty, satirical, subtle social critic without overtly coming out with a specific political message. In "Revolution," he broke this trend and started the first of his long line of political statements, although many of Lennon's songs portrayed other themes such as isolation, personal anxieties, love and sensuality, and lack of communication.

In 1968, when the Beatles copyrighted the lyrics to "Revolution" for the world, many New Left politicos protested that they had sold out the revolutionary movement and the consciousness for social change that the Beatles had helped to create.[1]

Some critics congratulated the Beatles for taking the sensible approach to social change and for rejecting New Left radical revolution. Others wondered if William F. Buckley hadn't written those status quo lyrics. Most of the record buyers, however, bought the song because they either liked it musically (the Beatle harmonies, Harrison's driving guitar) or because the Beatles had recorded it. Ironically, to add more controversy to the song, when the Beatles rerecorded "Revolution" on their *White Album*, Lennon indicated that he alone could be counted in for the revolution.

Lennon's political world view was moving to the left, and his songs started to reflect his political consciousness. He formed the Plastic Ono Band with Yoko Ono as a vehicle to express his political values and to make some new kinds of music. Lennon took strong stands against U.S. involvement in the Indochina war, and his basic cause soon became worldwide peace. At a time when few other artists cared, John Lennon and Yoko Ono were writing important antiwar songs like "Give Peace a Chance," which became an anthem for many antiwar protestors. John and Yoko had "bed-ins" for peace, they sent acorns to the leaders of the world to plant for peace, and they advertised worldwide in an effort to publicize peace. John and Yoko invested much capital and time to promote a new product that they hoped would be popular on the market: peace. Lennon cared at a time when the antiwar movement and the youth movement for social justice needed some response from their cultural heroes.

Lennon let people know where he stood on the issue of Vietnam. He began to take positions in his songs against capitalism, organized religion, mythical leaders, and the repressive state. In 1970, Lennon wrote his classic "Working Class Hero" for the *Plastic Ono Band* album.[2] He sang about a political system that turned the individual into a scared, unfeeling, political zombie. The system used dope, religion, and sex, along with television, to keep the working-class hero in a state of false bliss.

John Lennon put his political messages right out front. In another Lennon classic, "God," Lennon told us that the dream was over and that he did not believe in the old myths of leadership, religion, or pain diversions.[3] He said that he believed only in John and Yoko. All other leaders were false.

Since Richard Nixon was running for reelection in 1972, it is no coincidence that John Lennon's trouble with the U.S. Immigration and Naturalization Service began early in 1972. Lennon was seen as a threat to the Nixon administration since he was against war. Lennon had written that best-selling song, "Imagine," which received massive air play. Many pop singers on TV variety shows picked up on the song. "Imagine" was clearly the most radical political song ever to make the Top 40 charts. It is no wonder that Nixon, Agnew, Mitchell, and others were ready to deport Lennon.[4]

In 1971, Lennon had been associating with the likes of Jerry Rubin and Abbie Hoffman, promoting the idea of revolution. John and Yoko had not been exposed to the Rubin-Hoffman-type of "revolution for the media" familiar to most people in the movement in the late 1960s and early 1970s. When many veterans of the movement had grown tired of Jerry and Abbie's ideas John Lennon and Yoko Ono were just warming up to them.

Lennon and Yoko Ono became part of the politico/artistic scene in the Village as they tried to merge their art and politics. They did a benefit for former leader of the White Panther party, John Sinclair, who had been sent to jail for nine to ten years for possession of marijuana. Lennon and Ono started writing their most political songs, which would come out in 1972 in that totally political album, *Some Time in New York City*. They discussed with Rubin and Sinclair the possibilities of organizing political rock shows to tour the country, thus creating a new political consciousness in the youth cadres of America.[5] About his music, Lennon said, "People always talk about my music as if it's some new craze I'm into. Really it's been a natural evolution from 'All You Need Is Love' to 'Give Peace a Chance' to 'Power to the People' to 'Attica State.' "[6]

On the album *Some Time in New York City* were two woman's liberation movement songs ("Sisters, O Sisters" and "Woman Is the Nigger of the World"), two political prisoner songs ("Angela" and "John Sinclair"), two songs about repression in prison ("Attica State" and "Born in a Prison"), two songs about British repression in Northern Ireland ("The Luck of the Irish" and "Sunday Bloody Sunday"), one song about the "hip" life in New York ("New York City"), and one cosmic world-view song ("We're All Water"). John and Yoko did not miss a cause on this album. If it had been released in 1969 or 1970, *Some Time in New York City* would have knocked out the record industry and been a success commercially and politically. But in 1972, it was a dismal failure. It was political overkill with trite radical rhetoric as lyrics. Lennon was no longer giving subtle political messages backed by great musical compositions; rather he was singing overtly political songs that were for the most part poor musically. For all of Lennon's radical rhetoric on the album, the album cover carried a reminder to register to vote during the 1972 presidential election.

About the same time that Lennon was at his most political, the U.S. government began proceedings to deport him. On March 1, 1972, the Immigration and Naturalization Service granted Lennon the usual fifteen day extension on his visa pending further standard paperwork, then suddenly revoked the extension. Lennon, as it turned out, had been selectively chosen as a political example to the nation's youth, and he was beginning to feel the wrath of the Nixon-Agnew repression during the year of Watergate. In late February 1972, Senator Strom Thurmond (Rep., S.C.) sent the attorney general of the United States, John Mitchell, a note informing him of Lennon's plans to hold a massive peace demonstration at the 1972 Republican national convention, then planned for San Diego.[7] Repression soon followed.

The government classified Lennon as an "undesirable alien," since he had been convicted of possession of marijuana in 1968 in England. Lennon maintained that he had been set up by a British cop, who tried to plant dope on many rock stars to get publicity in busting them. He pled guilty to the charge in a deal with authorities. Probably of more concern to some U.S. government officials was Lennon's newfound radical political consciousness. He was a rock 'n' roll star, and he wasn't singing love lyrics. He was singing about repression in the United States, and his personal political actions were involved in protesting that repression in all its forms.

JOHN LENNON AND THE FBI

Lennon's file is a most incomplete and curious file. Pursuant to my request, 278 pages were reviewed by the agency and 186 pages were withheld in their entirety because of a host of exemptions that the FBI claimed, such as (b) (1), (b) (2), (b) (3), (b) (7) (C), and (b) (7) (D) (see the explanation of exemptions in figure 7.1). Much of the information that was released to me contained so many crucial deletions as to be almost meaningless. The parts of the file on Lennon that were intelligible deal with the 1972 period of Lennon political activity. These were the days when Lennon was hanging out with Jerry Rubin and singing antiwar and radical political songs. This was also the time that the government was trying to deport Lennon and Yoko Ono, and the files contain interesting exchanges on this legal problem. Finally, the most revealing aspect of the Lennon file is the involvement of the Nixon administration at the time, for the FBI routinely provided information to the "Honorable" H. R. Haldeman about Lennon's activities.

One source in the file told the FBI that "Lennon appears to be radically orientated, however he does not give the impression he is a true revolutionist since he is constantly under the influence of narcotics." Another memo said that the New York office had "several sources in a position to furnish information on subject's activities but sources do not have personal contact with the subject."

The FBI checked out a lead that Lennon was going to be appointed to the President's Council for drug abuse, and one memo from R. L. Shackelford to E.S. Miller on April 21, 1972, stated: "Irony of subject being appointed to President's Council for Drug Abuse, if true, is overwhelming since subject is currently reported heavy user of narcotics and frequently avoided by Rennie Davis and Jerry Rubin, convicted Chicago Seven Conspiracy trial defendants, due to his excessive use of narcotics."

The FBI and the Immigration and Naturalization Service also believed John and Yoko fabricated the story that Yoko's son from

Fig. 7.1.
Explanation of exemptions.
SUBSECTIONS OF TITLE 5, UNITED STATES CODE, SECTION 552

(b) (1) information which is currently and properly classified pursuant to Executive Order 12065 in the interest of the national defense or foreign policy, for example, information involving intelligence sources or methods

(b) (2) materials related solely to the internal rules and practices of the FBI

(b) (3) information specifically exempted from disclosure by statute (see continuation page)

(b) (4) privileged or confidential information obtained from a person, usually involving commercial or financial matters

(b) (5) inter-agency or intra-agency documents which are not available through discovery proceedings during litigation; documents, the disclosure of which would have an inhibitive effect upon the development of policy and administrative direction; or documents which represent the work product of an attorney-client relationship

(b) (6) materials contained in sensitive records such as personnel or medical files, the disclosure of which would constitute a clearly unwarranted invasion of personal privacy

(b) (7) investigatory records compiled for law enforcement purposes, the disclosure of which would: (A) interfere with law enforcement proceedings, including pending investigations; (B) deprive a person of the right to a fair trial or an impartial adjudication, or give one party of a controversy an undue advantage by exclusive access to such information; (C) constitute an unwarranted invasion of the personal privacy of another person; (D) reveal the identity of a confidential source or reveal confidential information furnished only by the confidential source; (E) disclose investigative techniques and procedures, thereby impairing their future effectiveness; and (F) endanger the life or physical safety of law enforcement personnel

111

a previous marriage, Kyoko Cox, had been abducted from Yoko by the father of the child. Some memos pursued this lead, but no one was able to show a plot by John and Yoko.

The FBI, H.R. Haldeman, and Richard Nixon worried about the possibility that Lennon would be part of activities to disrupt the 1972 convention in Miami. One memo from Special Agent Command in New York to the acting FBI director, dated July 27, 1972, said that Miami officials should note that "Lennon is reportedly a 'heavy user of narcotics' known as 'downers.' This information should be emphasized to local Law Enforcement Agencies covering MIREP, with regards to subject being arrested if at all possible on possession of narcotics charge." This memo indicates clearly that someone was out to arrest and "get" John Lennon. In another memo from the FBI data sheet on Lennon there exists a strange cartoon of Lennon proclaiming that "the pope smokes dope" (figure 7.2).

Finally, by December 8, 1972, a memo from New York to the acting director of the FBI with respect to John Lennon said, "In view of subject's inactivity in Revolutionary Activities and his seemingly rejection by NY Radicals, captioned case is being closed in the NY Division." But the memo continued: "In event other information comes to New York's attention indicating subject is active with Revolutionary groups, the case will be reopened at that time and the Bureau advised accordingly."

The Lennon files are still politically sensitive. Huge gaps exist and many CIA documents in FBI files on Lennon were withheld. However, what was released clearly indicates that some agents somewhere felt Lennon was a political threat, and they responded by gathering domestic intelligence on his activities and by clearly harassing his activities in the United States.

The following memos contain the secret to the Lennon harassment. Unfortunately, the FBI did not release the information contained within because of a (b) (1) exemption. I find it hard to believe that someone is still trying to use "national security" to protect the Nixon administration's political attacks on civil liberties in 1972, but evidently this is still a "hot" memo. Figures 7.3 and 7.4 show the memos to H.R. Haldeman and to the acting attorney general from the FBI director on April 25, 1972.

Fig. 7.2
Memo from F.B.I. data sheet.

John Winston Lennon

John Winston Lennon, a former member of the Beatles Rock Music Group is presently the subject of deportation hearing by the Immigration and Naturalization Service.

Lennon is described as follows:

Name: John Winston Lennon
Race: White
Date of Birth: October 9, 1940
Place of Birth: Liverpool, England
Hair: Brown to Blond
Weight: 160 pounds
Height: Approximately six feet
Build: Slender
Nationality: English
United States   105 Bank Street
Residence: New York City
Arrest Record: 1968 Narcotics Arrest, in
                         England for Possession of
                         Dangerous Drugs (Cannabis)
                         Pled Guilty

Fig. 7.3
Memo to H. R. Haldeman.

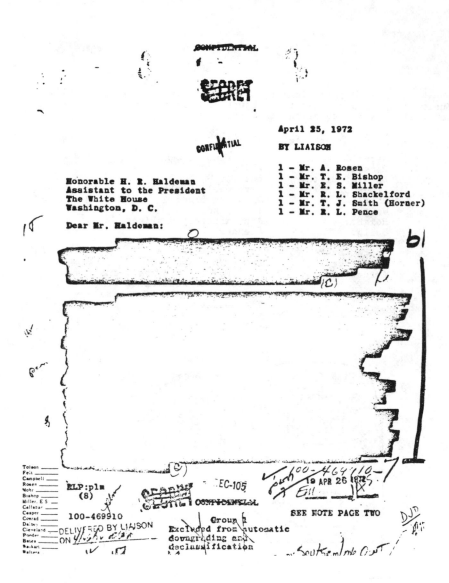

~~CONFIDENTIAL~~

~~SECRET~~

~~CONFIDENTIAL~~

April 25, 1972

BY LIAISON

1 – Mr. A. Rosen
1 – Mr. T. E. Bishop
1 – Mr. E. S. Miller
1 – Mr. R. L. Shackelford
1 – Mr. T. J. Smith (Horner)
1 – Mr. R. L. Pence

Honorable H. R. Haldeman
Assistant to the President
The White House
Washington, D. C.

Dear Mr. Haldeman:

Tolson
Felt
Campbell
Rosen
Mohr
Bishop
Miller, E S
Callahan
Casper
Conrad
Dalbey
Cleveland
Ponder
Bates
Baskart
Walters

ELP:plm
(8)

100-469910

DELIVERED BY LIAISON
ON

EC-105

100-469910-7

19 APR 26 1972

Group 1
Excluded from automatic
downgrading and
declassification

SEE NOTE PAGE TWO

114

(Fig. 7.3 continued)

CONFIDENTIAL

Honorable H. R. Haldeman   CONFIDENTIAL

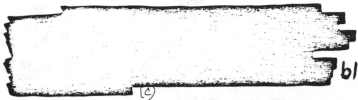

b1

(c)

This information is also being furnished to the
Acting Attorney General. Pertinent information concerning
Lennon is being furnished to the Department of State and INS
on a regular basis.

Sincerely yours,

NOTE:

b1

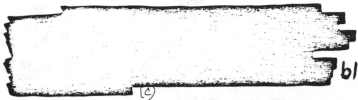

(c)

See memorandum R. L. Shackelford to Mr. E. S. Miller,
4/21/72, captioned "John Winston Lennon, Security Matter –
New Left," and prepared by RLP:plm.

CONFIDENTIAL

- 2 -

CONFIDENTIAL

CONFIDENTIAL

Fig. 7.4
Memo to the acting attorney general.

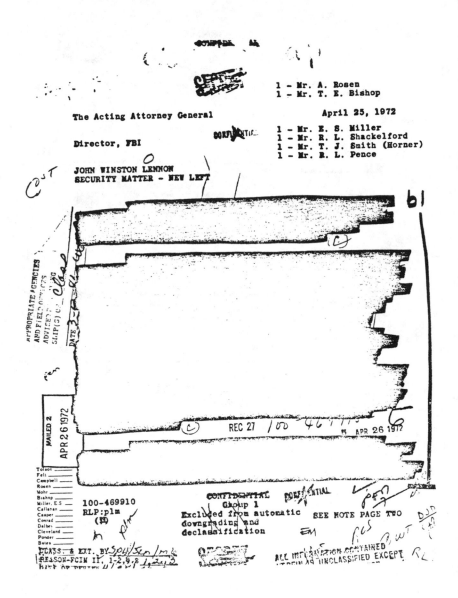

(Fig. 7.4 continued)

CONFIDENTIAL

The Acting Attorney General

CONFIDENTIAL

This information is also being furnished to the Honorable H. R. Haldeman, Assistant to the President, at The White House. Pertinent information concerning Lennon is being furnished to the Department of State and INS on a regular basis.

1 - The Deputy Attorney General

1 - Assistant Attorney General
    Internal Security Division

NOTE:

See memorandum R. L. Shackelford to Mr. E. S. Miller, 4/21/72, captioned as above, prepared by RLP:plm.

Lennon successfully fought the decision by the Immigration and Naturalization Service, and in a court battle he secured postponement of the final decision until 1974, when the Board of Immigration Appeals ordered Lennon to voluntarily leave the country by September 8, 1974, or he would be deported. Lennon filed suit because of the clear relation his case had to Watergate-related repression by the Nixon-Agnew administration. The outcome of this strange struggle between the U.S. government and a political rock star soon became clear. John Lennon won because he had staying power.

One thing that was clear in the struggle, however, was that the politico-artistic community was not united behind the struggle of John Lennon and Yoko Ono. Only *Rolling Stone* columnist Ralph Gleason was consistently outraged at the government's treatment of John Lennon. As early as June 1972, Gleason was trying to educate people about John Lennon's tenuous situation.[8] He was outraged and he called on all movement people of the 1960s and young people of the 1970s to unite around this crucial issue. The lack of response to Gleason's plea for organized protest should have given an indication of how well young people would organize and support a candidate like McGovern in the 1972 election.

Lennon and Post-Watergate Rock

John Lennon and Yoko Ono began having personal problems in 1973. The album that reflects this was *Mind Games*. It was little better artistically and musically than *Sometime in New York City*. John and Yoko declared the birth of a new nation called "Nutopia."[9] Most of the album was a revelation of John Lennon's "inner head," and that concept was getting a bit old. Lennon did write a semipolitical classic in "Bring on the Lucie (Freda Peeple)."

Some of Lennon's fans started to desert him after he began doing a number of strange things in public, such as appearing stoned and drunk at Los Angeles clubs, hassling the Smothers' Brothers during their show, and wearing a sanitary napkin on his head in a nightclub. His break-up with Yoko evidently affected him very hard. Yet he recovered spectacularly by producing perhaps the greatest post-Beatles album, *Walls and Bridges*.

This 1974 release confirmed that Lennon was still a musical genius. He had dropped most of his political rhetoric and was not as hostile as he had been before. Elton John and an assortment of superstars helped out on this great Lennon album, which proved that Lennon was still alive and well. It is an album about love relationships, and John and Yoko soon were together again.

John Lennon was the ultimate political rocker, and his assassination in December 1980 shocked the world. Lennon's death brought a spontaneous outpouring of grief from many Americans and inspired the largest mass mourning since the assassination of John F. Kennedy in 1963. Lennon's death symbolically signaled the end of political rock, and for many it was a sad reminder that the 1960s were indeed over. It was particularly tragic for his fans because he had just emerged from five years of self-imposed withdrawal from the rock star system. His message on his comeback album, *Double Fantasy*, was that he and Yoko Ono had survived the 1970s and were ready to take on the 1980s together. Moreover, his message on the album was one of caring, sharing, and being a whole person.

Lennon lived a nonsexist life, enjoyed being a father, and shared obligations and responsibilities fully with his lover and wife, Yoko Ono. Perhaps this was in some ways the most political message to come from any rocker since the glory days of political rock music, the early 1970s. Lennon maintained that a man should not be sexist and should support woman's liberation as the liberation of us all in the 1980s.

8 / Phil Ochs

IF PHIL OCHS, 1960s FOLK singer and politico, had been there, he would have loved the antinuclear weapons demonstrations in California and New York in the summer of 1982. He would have loved listening to Bob Dylan, Joan Baez, Jackson Browne, Bruce Springsteen, and others singing out and marching against nuclear weapons. In fact, Ochs probably would have been proud to march once again and to feel part of the nuclear freeze movement. Ochs was always looking for something to get into politically. He had covered the antinuclear weapons themes some twenty years earlier and would not have minded doing a few numbers in Central Park to protest the bombs. Unfortunately for movement politics and for the politics of popular music, Phil Ochs hanged himself on April 9, 1976.

This quintessential sixties person not only had a cult following of politicos, folk junkies, protest fans, and movement freaks but also had a "following" in the Federal Bureau of Investigation. In documents released under the Freedom of Information Act, it is clear that the FBI kept a domestic file on Ochs from 1963 until his suicide. As Ochs always said, "They [the government] have files on me this thick," and then he would laugh. He was absolutely correct. The FBI has released over four hundred pages from the Phil Ochs file, and it is clear from the documents that the FBI spent an extraordinary amount of time following, checking up on, and detailing the activities of Phil Ochs. The domestic political surveillance was initiated and kept in place because of Ochs's political beliefs and his political songs. Ochs was no laughing matter to the FBI. His main crime was that he thought "un-American" thoughts and sang "un-American" songs.

The first interest that the FBI showed in Phil Ochs came in a 1963 memo from SAC, New York, to the director of the FBI. This memo on subject Philip Ochs contained no New York office file number, of course, since it was the first report. The memo reads:

> "Mainstream," August, 1963, on page 34 contains a poem en-titled "Glory Bound" by Phil Ochs, and an article "The Guthrie Legacy" also by Ochs. Both the poem and the article are eulogies on folk singer and guitarist Woodie Guthrie, described as "incurably ill." Ochs does not specifically describe himself in these writings, but their content shows that he has conversed with guitarists and folk singers. The reader is drawn to conclude that Ochs himself is a guitarist and folk singer. An article on page 40 of the same issue "Mainstream" entitled "off the record" by Josh Dunson, describes Philip Ochs as a "topical song writer'." NYO Indices reflect no information concerning Philip Ochs.

Thus Ochs earlier "crimes" in the mind of an FBI agent had been staked out. He was a Woody Guthrie fan, he was a guitar player, topical singer, and songwriter, and he wrote in "Mainstream." With such information, the FBI started gathering data on Ochs and they would not stop until his death in 1976.

Agents checked Selective Service, insurance companies, the American Federation of Musicians Local 802 in New York, neighbors at 139 Thompson Street in New York City, the Credit Bureau of Greater New York, Bureau of Motor Vehicles, Bureau of Special Services, Board of Elections-Manhattan, and other sources. The only data the FBI came up with was that Ochs was a "beatnik type" and that he had not broken any laws or committed any crimes in New York City. The FBI then checked with an acquaintance of Ochs who resided in Greenwich Village who was a folksinger and guitarist. This person was also the subject of an FBI New York file, but the FBI did not press the subject for further information on Ochs when they discovered that the singer friend had suffered a mental breakdown and was confined to a mental institution.

The memo also revealed that the FBI agent noted that a Mr. Bob Dylan was also mentioned in the August 1963 issue of "Mainstream." Dylan was also referred to as a folksinger and a "topical songwriter." No doubt the FBI started a file then on Robert Zimmerman—Bob Dylan—just as they had for Ochs.

By February 16, 1966, Ochs still had not reached the status of an all-out radical subversive in the eyes of the FBI. In a memo to Director J. Edgar Hoover from SAC, New York, it was noted that two confidential sources had advised the FBI that Ochs entertained at a rally on April 23, 1964, at Cooper Union, New York, sponsored by the Committee to Secure Justice for Morton Sobell and that Ochs "sang topical folk songs at a street rally protesting the United States participation in the war in Viet Nam" on October 15, 1965, in Philadelphia. Even though the New York office considered the Morton Sobell committee to be a communist front group since Sobell was a codefendent of Ethel and Julius Rosenberg in 1953, and even though Ochs had sung antiwar songs during the Vietnam war, the New York office advised that further action with respect to Phil Ochs "does not appear warranted at this time." It was also noted that Ochs had connections with Disaster Relief to Cuba (emergency committee), Greater New York Labor Press Club (The Worker), New York Council to Abolish the House Un-American Activities committee, Progressive Labor party, and Progressive Labor movement. Ochs not only sang topical songs, but in the eyes of the FBI, he was an activist.

The next important memo in the Ochs file was from J. Edgar Hoover to the SAC, New York office, dated October 1, 1968. Hoover asked the New York office to bring up to date the file on the activities of Philip Ochs in relation to the Democratic national convention and the antiriot laws. Hoover warned, "During your investigation remain particularly alert to subject's writings and public statements which would indicate his attitude toward violence to attain anti-United States objectives." The office was to furnish an evaluation as to whether Ochs was to be included in the Security Index.

The Los Angeles FBI office investigated Ochs from August 31 to December 12, 1968, and forwarded data to the New York office, which answered Hoover's query by responding that Ochs should be in the Security Index. In late 1968, Director Hoover informed the U.S. Secret Service that Phil Ochs was a security matter for the "presidential protection program" for a number of reasons. Hoover said Ochs "is potentially dangerous; or has been identified as a member or participant in communist movement; or has been under active investigation as member of other group or organization inimical to U.S." Moreover, Ochs fell into a category of "subversives" who by prior acts (including arrests or convictions) "or conduct or statements" indicated a "propensity for violence and antipathy toward good order and government." The FBI had moved Ochs from harmless folksinger to possible presidential killer with one swift memo.

The data gathering and information in the files on Ochs's background grew immensely after his participation in the demonstrations in Chicago at the Democratic convention in 1968. If the FBI thinks you might be a potential killer of the president, they must get loads of background data. The FBI talked to officials at Ohio State University and found that Ochs was born on December 19, 1940, in El Paso, Texas, and that his father was Jacob Ochs, a doctor in Columbus, Ohio. Ohio State also reported that Ochs attended from September 1958 to March 1962. Michael Ochs, Phil's brother, advised that as of September 27, 1968, Phil Ochs lived with him in Topanga, California. A and M Record Company advised the FBI that Ochs was employed by them, and background data showed Ochs had been arrested during his college days at Rivera Beach, Florida, for "vagrancy" and in West Palm Beach, Florida, for "possession of alcoholic beverages by a minor" in 1960. Ochs FBI number was 479 841 D. He was also arrested by Chicago police on August 23, 1968, for disorderly conduct and by Los Angeles police on August 30,

1967, for a misdemeanor traffic warrant. Moreover, the Communist Front Group Activity listing included the groups mentioned earlier in this section with the addition of the May Day celebrations. Evidence of Och's Communist party sympathy included his eulogies for Woody Guthrie. The final supporting evidence in the documents that labeled Ochs as a security threat contain all of the miscellaneous activities that the FBI was able to gather.

On October 15, 1965, Phil Ochs, a folk singer, who at that time was appearing at the Second Fret, a night club and coffee house in Philadelphia, was observed by SAS of the FBI to entertain at a "speak-out" held at City Hall, Philadelphia, Pa., sponsored by the Philadelphia Area Committee to End the War in Vietnam.

"The Worker" of January 9, 1966, page four, contained an article disclosing "Phil Ochs sang about the war" at a teach-in sponsored by the Student Non-violent Coordinating Committee and Students for Peace in Vietnam, an affiliate of Students for a Democratic Society (SDS) held December 29, 1965, at Columbia University's McMillin Auditorium, NY City. The article stated, "The teach-in was aimed at high school students and was an attempt to organize and give expression to high school sentiment... on the war in Vietnam." ("The Worker" is an east coast Communist newspaper that ceased publication in July, 1968....)

"The Worker" of April 11, 1967, page one, column four, indicated Phil Ochs was one of the artists scheduled to participate in the April 15, 1967, anti-Vietnam demonstration in New York City sponsored by the Spring Mobilization Committee to End the War in Vietnam (SMC).

The October 16, 1967, issue of "Mobilization News," published by the National Mobilization Committee to End the War in Vietnam (NMC), listed Phil Ochs as one of the entertainers who would appear at the October 21, 1967, anti-Vietnam demonstration at the Pentagon in Washington, D.C.

The October 27, 1967, issue of the "Kingsman," a Brooklyn College, Brooklyn, New York, newspaper, reflected that Phil Ochs was one of the folk singers who performed at the October 21, 1967, anti-Vietnam demonstration at the Pentagon, Washington, D.C.

The November 23, 1967, issue of "The Village Voice," a New York City newspaper, contained an article written by Phil Ochs captioned, "Have You Heard? The War Is Over!" In this article the author calls for a rally in Washington Square Park, New York City, on November 25, 1967, to declare an end to the Vietnam war.

The November 26, 1967, issue of the "New York Times," a daily New York City newspaper, contained a report of an impromptu march of several thousand persons from an anti-Vietnam rally at Washington Square Park, New York City, to Times Square and the United Nations, New York City, on November 25, 1967. The article indicated, "The original idea for the anti-war demonstration started with Phil Ochs, a composer and singer, who has been called 'a troubadour of the New Left.'" The article continued, "He had organized a similar march in Los Angeles last summer and subsequently wrote a satirical song on 'the war is over' concept. But Mr. Ochs, after appearing at Washington Square shortly before 1 o'clock, refused to join the march when that suggestion caught on."

The January 22, 1968, issue of the "Newark Evening News," a Newark, New Jersey, daily newspaper, page three, reflected that Phil Ochs was one of the performing artists at the Broadway for Peace 1968 presentation at Lincoln Center, New York City, January 21, 1968, sponsored by the Congressional Peace Campaign Committee.

The February 15, 1968, issue of "Win," a publication of the War Resisters League in cooperation with the New York Workshop for Nonviolence, carried on page fifteen, an article entitled, "The Birth of the Yippies." The piece reflects the Youth International Party (YIP) was founded in New York City on January 16, 1968, by some 25 artists, writers and revolutionaries, including Phil Ochs.

The February 27, 1968, issue of the "Long Island Press," a metropolitan New York City newspaper, contained an article reporting an interview with Keith Lampe, a founder of YIP, wherein Lampe said that among those involved in creating YIP was folk singer Phil Ochs.

The March 21, 1968, issue of the "Village Voice," contained an article indicating that Phil Ochs joined the original four founders of YIP as an organizer.

The "Village Voice," a New York City newspaper, on March 7, 1968, page twenty-eight, contained an article reflecting Phil Ochs would be one of the entertainers at a benefit for the National Committee for Free Elections in Mississippi on that date at the Tavern-on-the Green in New York City.

"The Worker" of April 23, 1968, page one, column two, disclosed that Phil Ochs was one of the folk singers scheduled to appear at the April 27, 1968, anti-Vietnam demonstration in Central Park, New York City, sponsored by the Fifth Avenue Vietnam Peace Parade Committee.

On August 23, 1968, a SA of the FBI observed a demonstration at the Civic Center Plaza, Chicago, Illinois, and observed approximately 50 youths where a YIP press conference was scheduled for 10:15 a.m. on that date.

At 10:20 a.m. it was observed that a live pig was brought to the Plaza by the YIP contingent which they announced was the YIP "candidate" for President of the United States. When efforts were made by the Chicago Police to bring the pig under control, 7 Yippies attempted to intervene and were arrested by the police. One of those so arrested was Phil Ochs, a white male, born December 19, 1940.

When Ochs was arrested by the Chicago police because he was interfering with the arrest of a live pig, the FBI began to investigate all aspects of Ochs's life. They hoped that he could be prosecuted as one of the Chicago defendents for the conspiracy trials relating to the Democratic national convention.

It was Ochs's strange luck to have spent the nights before the Democratic national convention with an FBI informant, William D. McCuaig, who volunteered his apartment to demonstrators through the office of the underground radical Chicago newspaper, *The Seed*. McCuaig then talked to the FBI after Ochs, Wolfe Lowenthal, Jerry Rubin, and Abby Hoffman left his apartment.

The bureau checked San Francisco, Los Angeles, Chicago, and even Cincinnati FBI field offices for more information on Ochs. The Cincinnati office volunteered some new information that had escaped the FBI: Ochs was against nuclear bombs. He had sung peace songs for the Women's International League of Peace and Freedom, Columbus, Ohio, chapter, in January 1962.

The memo in figure 8.1 contains the earliest reference to Ochs's activities.

Much more information was generated in the Ochs file. The FBI would leave no stone unturned. The following data was gathered:

On April 5, 1969, Special Agents of the Federal Bureau of Investigation (FBI) observed the GI-Civilian Anti-War Parade and Rally, and reported that at approximately 4:45 PM, Phil Ochs was introduced by the Chairman, and sang a song titled "On March 10, the Battle of New Orleans ———." This was followed by another song by Ochs called "All Quiet in the Western Front."

"The New York Times," a New York City daily newspaper, in its issue of April 6, 1969, on page one contained an article captioned "Thousands March Here to Demand Vietnam Pull Out." This article stated that thousands of anti-war demonstrators marched along the Avenue of the Americas on April 5, 1969, from Bryant Park to Central Park for a rally in "a downpour" demanding United States withdrawal from Vietnam, chanting, "End the war in Vietnam," "Bring the troops home," and "Free speech for GI's." The article noted that this parade began a weekend of anti-war demonstrations here (New York City) and in Chicago, Los Angeles, San Francisco, Seattle.

Informants generally familiar with SCDCP activity and associated front group activity in the area where Ochs resides advised that they have no information concerning any membership or current SCDCP activity or front group activity on the part of Ochs.

The "Daily Trojan," campus newspaper at the University of Southern California, Los Angeles, California, October 16, 1969, carried a photograph of Phil Ochs who had ended a year-long retirement the previous day at the University of Southern California (USC) in a benefit performance for the Vietnam Moratorium Committee. He had also appeared at three other college campuses in the Los Angeles area during the day. This was described as his first activity since the Democratic convention in Chicago.

The Vietnam Moratorium Committee had been publicly described as a national group headquartering in Washington, D.C., formed for the purpose of calling a "moratorium on business as usual" in protest of the Vietnam war.

The FBI even included an interview that Ochs gave to *Ramparts* that was published August 24, 1968. This was supposed to

Fig. 8.1
Memo.

UNITED STATES DEPARTMENT OF JUSTICE

FEDERAL BUREAU OF INVESTIGATION

Cincinnati, Ohio
October: 2 , 1968

*In Reply, Please Refer to
File No.*

CONFIDENTIAL

RE: PHILIP DAVID OCHS

The January, 1962, Columbus Branch newsletter
of the Women's International League for Peace and Freedom
stated that Philip Ochs sang peace songs at a meeting of the
Universalist Church in Columbus, Ohio, on January 6, 1962.
From the church the group went to the downtown area, the
Fairgrounds where President John F. Kennedy was to speak,
and to the airport. The group carried signs and distributed
leaflets urging, "No Resumption of Nuclear Testing in the
Atmosphere", "Keep Nuclear Arms From NATO","Staff the National
Arms Control and Disarmament Agency As Soon As Possible".

Women's International League For Peace
and Freedom - Columbus, Ohio, Chapter

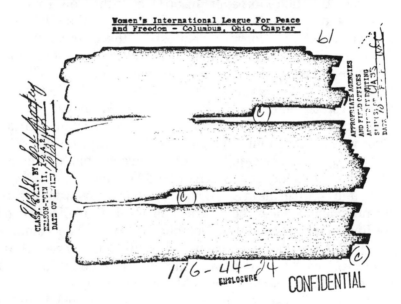

176-44-24

ENCLOSURE

CONFIDENTIAL

129

be evidence of his personal political beliefs, but the memo in figure 8.2 indicates that there was still not enough evidence against Ochs to prosecute him.

It seemed that everyone was willing to talk to the FBI about Phil Ochs except Ochs! He refused to be interrogated by FBI agents on October 1, 1968. Unlike some of his friends and acquaintances, Ochs felt the FBI had no right to ask him questions about his activities. He had broken no law. Indeed, his only "crime" appears to be that he offended Hoover's sense of American patriotic behavior.

By 1969 Ochs had added a new arrest to his list. He was busted for possession of marijuana on October 5, 1968, by the Los Angeles police department. This was at the time the Los Angeles FBI office was reporting on Ochs to the New York FBI office, and they were to prepare a report on whether Ochs was a subversive as per Hoover's request. In the October 20, 1968, report by SAC, New York, to the FBI director, the agency for the first time classified Ochs as a Communist by putting an "x" next to that category. This was done in spite of evidence that Ochs was not a Communist or even a Marxist. He never joined the Communist party. But now the agency was certain that since Ochs was a "Communist sympathizer" and since he was subversive" and "un-American," it would be acceptable to label him a "Communist." Only one informer said he was.

As if to confirm his original notion that Ochs was dangerous to the president, Hoover received a report from the FBI office in Little Rock, Arkansas, dated October 22, 1969. The memo was titled "Rehearsals for Retirement by Phil Ochs, *Threat Against the President*." A woman had complained to the Little Rock FBI office that her fourteen-year-old son had bought a Phil Ochs record at a drugstore. The report from Little Rock noted that Ochs threatened the life of the president in a song called "Pretty Smart on My Part." Hoover now thought he was correct about Phil Ochs.

In 1970 the FBI file added the Youth International party, or Yippies, to the list of Ochs's affiliated groups, and Ochs was busted again in Los Angeles for disorderly conduct. The FBI had three sets of Ochs's fingerprints, his arrest record, his group affiliations and the history of those groups, and surveillance

Fig. 8.2
Memo.

UNITED STATES DEPARTMENT OF JUSTICE
FEDERAL BUREAU OF INVESTIGATION

Copy to:	2 - USA., Chicago

b7C

Report of: SA ~~███████████~~ Office: Chicago, Illinois
Date: December 5, 1968

Field Office File #: 176-50   Bureau File #: 176-44

Title: PHILIP DAVID OCHS

Character: ANTIRIOT LAWS

Synopsis: Interview of OCHS in 8/24/68, issue of "Ramparts Wallposter" set forth. AUSA, Chicago, declined to consider prosecution of OCHS.

- C -

ALL INFORMATION CONTAINED
HEREIN IS UNCLASSIFIED
DATE ___ BY ___

131

reports on Ochs. He was observed by a New York special agent departing Kennedy airport with Jerry Rubin for Paris, France, on October 25, 1970.

By 1971, J. Edgar Hoover recognized the mistake in labelling Phil Ochs a "Communist." Hoover sent a memo to SAC, Los Angeles, on April 27, 1971, saying:

> Subject's Security Index (SI) card at Bureau shows tabbing of "communist." This is in conflict with scope of subject's current activities, revealing substantial association and participation in the affairs of Youth International Party (YIP). In view of the above, submit FD-122 to Bureau recommending subject's SI card be revised to show affiliation with YIP.

The SAC Los Angeles office quickly responded to Hoover's directive by resubmitting Phil Ochs's classification as "Miscellaneous —Youth International party" in a memo of April 29, 1971. Thus Ochs's "Communist" past, that is, the FBI misclassification, was erased. However, this did not mean that Ochs would be removed as a security threat. His file was reevaluated and because of his "participation and gratuitous entertainment services as a folk singer at various militant left wing activities as recently as April 1971, coupled with the fact that he was reportedly one of the four founders of the Youth International party as an organizer," the study recommended that Ochs remain in the Security Index listing. And again, J. Edgar Hoover notified the Secret Service, July 30, 1971, that Phil Ochs was a concern in the protection of the president.

Ochs's FBI file included some new group affiliations by 1971, such as the Liberation Union or Friends of the Black Panthers, National Peace Action Coalition, the Newton-Cleaver Defense Committee, and the Vietnam Moratorium Committee.

In December 1971, the FBI, the State Department, and the legal attache at Buenos Aires were all sharing information about Phil Ochs because Ochs and David Ifshin had visited Bolivia and other places in South America. In 1972 the FBI was still using "suitable pretext" to gain information about Ochs. Ochs had added another arrest by 1972, this one on December 12, 1971, in Los Angeles, for driving under the influence of alcohol. He retained his label as "subversive." In July 1972, the acting director of the FBI, L. Patrick Gray, took up where Hoover had left off by saying in a memo that Ochs was "potentially dangerous because of background, emotional instability, or activity in groups engaged in activities inimical to U.S."

In 1973 the agency added Ochs's phone number to their computerized telephone file and classified him as "extremist" and "subversive" with respect to his foreign travel. In 1975 Ochs was arrested, as alias "John B. Train," for burglary, assault, and criminal mischief by the NYPD. This was the final arrest in his FBI record. There is no evidence that Ochs was removed from FBI Security Matter classification even though he did not engage in any security threats or movement political activity for most of the 1970s.

The FBI files on Phil Ochs finally were closed because of his suicide in 1976. The director of the FBI was informed by the Los Angeles office that the *Los Angeles Times* reported "subject of investigation" was dead. The New York FBI office also informed the director that the *New York Times* had reported Ochs's death. Director of the FBI Clarence M. Kelley noted that Ochs was dead. Yet on May 5, 1976, the director submitted the name of Phil Ochs to the Secret Service "concerning protective responsibilities" for the president. Kelley checked the box that said Ochs was "potentially dangerous because of background, emotional instability or activity in groups engaged in activities inimical to U.S." and he provided a picture of Phil Ochs. This was done almost one month after Phil Ochs died. Director Kelley then informed the Secret Service that there had been reports of Ochs's death.

The final entry in the Ochs file is something Phil would have appreciated more than most people. It involves a request by the legal attache in London for current information about the activities of Phil Ochs. The request is dated May 24, 1977, over one year after his death. The Los Angeles office then informed the foreign liason unit on August 13, 1977, that Ochs was dead. The message was clear—stop blaming Phil Ochs for everything. He is dead!

9/Rock Politicos

DAVID CROSBY, STEVEN STILLS, GRAHAM Nash, and Neil Young were political rockers of the late 1960s and early 1970s. They combined some political lyrics in a few songs with top quality rock music to emerge as the social conscience of the Woodstock Nation. This was the "supergroup" of the late 1960s and early 1970s, filling the void left after the Beatles split up. Each was a star in his own right (Nash with the Hollies background, Crosby with the Byrds experience, and Stills and Young with the Buffalo Springfield), and together they made some of the best music ever to come out of rockdom.

STEVEN STILLS

Stills wrote the Buffalo Springfield classic "For What It's Worth" in 1966. Rock critic Richard Goldstein said about Stills: "Stephen Stills composed this protest anthem following a youth riot on the Sunset Strip. ('Heat' is California slang for cops....) It has since been regarded as a broader statement on the nature of hip resistance. Stills seems to counsel dignified passivity based on a faith in the inevitability of change. 'We'll outlive them,' his song seems to say. 'See—we've won already.' "[1]

Stills wrote about paranoia on the strip in Los Angeles, and about confrontations between police and the young people.[2] Later on, when Stills was touring with Crosby, Nash, and Young, he updated and revived "For What It's Worth" and sang it to the antiwar crowds that the group drew. Stills turned the song into a loud piano rock number and he added a new twist to the song, "the rock ranting and raving" technique.

Stills "ranted and raved" to this politically conscious audience during the group's 1970 summer tour, which came just after the invasion of Cambodia, the murders at Kent State, Jackson State, and the May student strikes. Stills's political rantings were one of the highlights of that tour.

Stills was often quoted as saying that "politics is bullshit," but he continued writing political songs in the 1970s. He wrote "Find the Cost of Freedom"[3] and a song to humanity, "We Are Not Helpless, We Are Men," performed on his first solo album.

GRAHAM NASH

If Stills was the quintessential rock'n'roll man, with his flashy guitar and groupies, Graham Nash appeared as the quiet, sensitive one of the group. "Willie" Nash seemed a little removed from the Sunset Strip, rock'n'roll trip that Stills, Young, and Crosby had been through. Nash was a veteran of the Hollies with their many great pop rock hits of the 1960s.

Nash was a splendid songwriter, with special talents as a political-rock composer. He wrote "Chicago," "Military Madness," "Southbound Train," and many others. His albums *Songs for Beginners* and *Wild Tales* both contain a number of political songs that stress equality, freedom, and fraternity. Unfortunately, the albums did not do well, and Nash did not reach as wide an audience as he would have liked.

Nash is probably revered by his fans more for "Our House" and "Teach Your Children" than for his political songs. Surely one of the highlights of the group's 1970 tour was in Chicago when they sang Nash's song "Chicago" at the Auditorium.[4] Before a Chicago audience that included many veterans from the 1968 struggle at the Democratic convention, Nash introduced the song by saying, "This is a song for Mayor Daley." Then he broke into "Chicago," a song that told the story of Richard Daley's repressive political machine as evidenced by the events at the convention and by the police riot. Graham "Willie" Nash would not soon be forgotten by that crowd.

DAVID CROSBY

David Crosby had long had a reputation as a rock politico from his early days with the Byrds and his association with Roger McGuinn. For the group's first album, *Crosby, Stills and Nash,* Crosby combined with Stills to write a futuristic classic, "Wooden Ships," about a nuclear holocaust. Crosby also added "Long Time Gone" after Robert Kennedy's assassination, which became a theme for the Woodstock ethos.[5]

Crosby often warned against forces he referred to as "them." Onstage he would talk about a conspiracy to assassinate John Kennedy, because he did not believe the Warren Report. In retrospect, given the revelation of the Pentagon Papers and the Watergate scandal, Crosby's fears seem justified. In his paranoiac classic, "Almost Cut My Hair," Crosby screamed out his message after introducing the song in Chicago-police style, "I will now proceed to entangle the entire area."

Crosby was highly political onstage when he toured with Nash in 1973. He talked about Watergate and repression, and sang old political songs, like Neil Young's "Ohio."[6] In fact, when Crosby and Nash were called back for an encore, they often performed "Ohio." Crosby was surely the "loving freak" of CSNY, and his political consciousness was probably the most radical in the group.

NEIL YOUNG

The best songwriter/poet of the group was Neil Young. Young was with the Buffalo Springfield before he began a solo career. He had written such Springfield classics as "Mr. Soul," "On the Way Home," "Nowadays Clancy Can't Even Sing," "Broken Arrow," "I Am a Child," and "Expecting to Fly." He was an intense songwriter who painted deep personal images in his works.

In Young's first solo album he established the themes of going back to the country and of ecology. In his second solo album with Crazy Horse, *Everybody Knows This Is Nowhere,* Young

introduced "Down by the River" and "Cowgirl in the Sand." He
was known as one of the best of the new songwriters of the late
1960s.

In 1970, Young became much more political in his songwriting.
He wrote the definitive political statement relating to the antiwar movement and the student movement of 1969-1971 when he
wrote "Ohio." That song was to its generation of politicized
students what Bob Dylan's "Blowin' in the Wind" was to the civil
rights movement. Young wrote the song after hearing about the
Kent State killings.

When Crosby, Stills, Nash, and Young first performed the
song live during their 1970 tour, they sounded as if they were
ready to defend themselves with their powerful electric guitars
against "tin soldiers and Nixon coming." Four years later, when
the group reunited for the 1974 tour, "Ohio" would still bring
back these feelings.

In 1970, Young wrote other political songs, like "Southern
Man," which dealt with white racism and repression of blacks in
the South.[7] Later, in 1974, that down-home southern rockin'
band from Alabama, Lynyrd Skynyrd, would answer Young's
charges in a song called "Sweet Home Alabama."[8] Those were
appropriate come-back lyrics for the southern band since 1974
was Boston's year as the "Selma of the North."

Young's *After the Gold Rush* album was another milestone.[9]
The title song was curious in that it offered the listener any
number of possible interpretations. The song was either about a
nuclear holocaust or an ecological disaster in the future, or an
account of a dope-induced trip by Young. No matter which inter-
pretation one chose, the song had impact.

Young's influence on rock from 1969 to 1971 was strong. He
sent a whole generation of songwriters into new areas that he
had probed both lyrically and musically. While Dylan was
remaining relatively quiet during this period, Young captured
the role as a spokesperson for his generation. For many of his
fans, he would never relinquish that role, even after Dylan
emerged again in 1974.

In 1973, Young had an off-year musically. He toured the country with the Stray Gators, who had helped him make the commercially successful *Harvest*. But onstage, Young was at times a

tragic figure. He would miss notes, stop in the middle of songs, blow guitar riffs, and sometimes lose his voice. Some of the low spots of that sad tour were recorded in Young's 1973 album called *Time Fades Away*. The album captures a burned-out superstar during a low point in his career: it was the worst album that Neil Young put out.

By 1974, many of Neil Young's fans were worried about what had happened to "Superstar Number One." But Young showed them in *On the Beach* that he had it all back together—better than ever. It was surely the best thing Young had done since *After the Gold Rush* in the early 1970s. *On The Beach* was released during the Nixon-resignation summer of 1974. It was the definitive political statement by a rock artist during the Watergate years 1972-1974. Young had taken us through a series of changes: broken arrows, Mr. Soul, cowgirls in the sand, back to nature, searching for hearts of gold, plaid shirts, buckskin jackets, after the gold rush, and four dead in Ohio. Now he was around to help pull us through the depression of the Watergate years. Young put together the most depressing yet true statement about the idealistic 1960's youth movement. It was the story of the hopeful child of the 1960s who had to face the harsh reality of living in the 1970s.

On the Beach contains two masterpieces in "Revolution Blues" and "Ambulance Blues." Young alludes to Charles Manson and the Patricia Hearst case among other headline stories in his songs. He gives us his reasons for withdrawing into seclusion in "On the Beach." In the long "Ambulance Blues" which closes the album, Young sings one of the most depressing songs ever recorded. In it he summarizes his entire political and musical past.

On the album's cover is a discarded newspaper carrying the headline "Sen. Buckley calls for Nixon to Resign." For Young this symbolized the Watergate story and the end of Richard Nixon. His album was the main political album that came out of the "post-revolutionary period" after the Watergate crisis. It was one of the few political rock albums in the period 1972-1974, and it signaled the last effort for the rock politicos in this period. Political rock music had been dying down in correspondence to the decline of movement protests in the United States, and it was

Young, one of the founders of political rock, who put the finishing touches on that period.

Finally, it was Neil Young who ushered in the 1980s for all rock politicos with a return to lyrics that made some political statements in his 1980 album called *Hawks and Doves*. Young remained a sensitive songwriter who recognized that hawks and doves were ready to go at it again during the Reagan administration and during America's newfound patriotism.

ROGER MCGUINN AND THE BYRDS

Another rock politico of considerable importance was Roger McGuinn of the Byrds. The Byrds were probably the best American rock'n'roll band of the 1960s and were important because they spread Bob Dylan's fame to a popular audience. The Byrds started folk rock by electrifying Dylan's song, "Mr. Tambourine Man." The Byrds were the first rock group to do "space rock" music, and they established themselves as leaders in the raga genre, complete with Indian sitar. McGuinn was a leader in using Moog synthesizers and, of course, the Byrds were the ones who started the whole country-rock scene.

The Byrds began their political rock career by performing a few of Dylan's songs, but later McGuinn started writing his own political songs. Some of the group's earlier work included Dylan's "Chimes of Freedom" and "My Back Pages." The Byrds also did "Turn, Turn, Turn." McGuinn wrote a political tribute to John Kennedy titled "He Was a Friend of Mine," which dealt with the singer's feelings of sadness at the loss of a "friend" who had been assassinated in Dallas. McGuinn and fellow Byrd Gram Parsons wrote a classic tribute to rednecks in "Drug Store Truck Drivin' Man."[10] The images captured in this song rank with Merle Haggard's "Okie from Muskogee."

Besides paving the way for the use of psychedelics with songs like "Eight Miles High" and "5-D," McGuinn was a master of social satire. He and Jaques Levy wrote the classic "I Wanna Grow Up to Be a Politician."[11]

Other Byrd members were highly influenced by McGuinn's political style, although the most political Byrd, David Crosby, left the group early after some disagreements with McGuinn.

Later, fellow Byrd Skip Battin and his glitter-rock friend Kim Fowley wrote "America's Great National Pastime"[12] and a socio-political commentary on the 1930s called "Citizen Kane."

The Byrds, under the direction of McGuinn, were an important force in rock music. McGuinn established himself as a rocker with a social conscience. Even after the Byrds broke up and McGuinn started putting out solo albums, he retained this special force.

10/More Politicos and the FBI

THE FREEDOM OF INFORMATION ACT is a useful tool for gathering information that the government might have on certain individuals and topics, even though it has too many loopholes and exemptions to allow for a truly free flow of information. Moreover, the use of the FOIA is certainly not free. Depending on which government agency is involved in a particular information search, the cost can be prohibitive. Knowing this, I filed FOIA requests with the Federal Bureau of Investigation and the Central Intelligence Agency in November 1981 to gather information on "the politics of rock music." My letter said: "I would like to ascertain the existence of certain files, investigative reports and documents that the Federal Bureau of Investigation [or CIA] may have collected from 1955 to 1979 that relate to rock music, rock music artists and groups, and the politics of rock music. Moreover, if any files exist, I would like to have a copy of such files if the cost is not too prohibitive. Please advise if you have any files, reports, and/or documents at the main office of the FBI or in the field offices that would be available to me under the Freedom of

Information Act concerning the following rock music artists and topics." I included a list of sixty-nine persons, groups, events, and publications.

The CIA response from John E. Bacon, information and privacy coordinator, was swift. The agency would be willing to look through their files for my names of rock fame if I supplied them with an average $90 per item search charge. Thus my FOIA request of sixty-nine items would cost about $6,210, and there would be no guarantee that what I requested would be in the files. Bacon requested a check of $3,000 to show my good faith so the searches could begin. Finally Bacon advised me that "it is highly unlikely that our files would contain much, if any, information relevant to your request. The CIA is a foreign intelligence organization." Evidently Bacon had not heard of the revelation of CIA domestic spying by Seymour Hersh and others in the 1970s. Besides, many of the people on my rock list were not U.S. citizens.

I was required to supply notarized releases from living third parties, and I had to give the full names, dates and places of birth, citizenship, whether or not they were deceased, and any other data that might identify the persons on my list. Without this information, I was warned, the search costs would be much higher!

Since I did not have the ability to get releases and autographs from the living rock stars such as Bob Dylan and Mick Jagger, and because I did not want to pay CIA over $6,000 for a search that might yield nothing, I decided to drop my CIA FOIA request. (Who knows what might lurk in the files of the CIA with respect to the politics of rock music?)

The FBI, on the other hand, turned out to be very cooperative, and they produced a gold mine of files. James K. Hall (chief, Freedom of Information-Privacy Acts Section, Records Management Division, U.S. Department of Justice, FBI) first informed me that I would need notarized releases for any living rock stars to get their records if any such records existed. He also informed me that I could have access to FBI files of dead rock stars. Hall noted, "Although we are aware some of the persons mentioned by you in your reference letter are deceased, such as Elvis Presley and John Lennon, we would like to ask you to inform us of the identities of the others who may be deceased."

It was lucky for me that there is no lack of dead rock stars from 1955 to 1979 to select from. I resubmitted my FOIA request to the FBI asking for the files and documents on Jimi Hendrix, Elvis Presley, Lowell George, Richard Farina, Harry Chapin, Jim Morrison, Phil Ochs, Janis Joplin, Bob Marley, John Lennon, and Sid Vicious. I figured that this was a reasonable start, but I had no idea how many pages would be revealed and what the charge would be for me to look at them.

In March 1982, James Hall told me that the FBI did not have any files or information at all on Lowell George, Richard Farina, Harry Chapin, or Bob Marley. These artists had never been the subject of an FBI investigation according to Hall. I could have access to the following: Phil Ochs, 429 pages; John Lennon, 92 pages; Jim Morrison, 91 pages; Elvis Presley, 87 pages; Jimi Hendrix, 7 pages; Janis Joplin, 1 page. The pages would cost ten cents per page, which brought the FBI charges to $70.70. Hall also wrote in his March letter that "documents have been located concerning Sid Vicious, and they will be assigned for processing in the near future." I quickly sent my check for $70.70 to the FBI.

By the end of April 1982, I had received the files on Ochs, Lennon, Presley, Morrison, Hendrix, and Joplin. The file on Sid Vicious (John Simon Ritchie) was withheld in its entirety to protect material that is exempted from disclosure by the following subsection of Title 5, United States Code, Section 552:

(b) (1) information which is currently and properly classified pursuant to Executive Order 12065 in the interest of the national defense or foreign policy;

(b) (7) investigatory reports compiled for law enforcement purposes, the disclosure of which would:

(C) constitute an unwarranted invasion of the personal privacy of another person.

Here then is my review of the FBI files I received.

JANIS JOPLIN

Joplin made it into the FBI files because she was the featured act at a concert in Ravinia Park at which the Chicago field office of the FBI thought violence might erupt. The memo is marked "To Director," "From Chicago," and it is labeled "Urgent." Some "reliable source" had indicated that the Ravinia Park concert in

Highland Park, Illinois, on August 5, 1970, would be disrupted by violence by "unknown persons, possibly some of those involved in disruption of Chicago Grant Park rock concert, July 27, '70." The source further advised the director that the concert was to be "patrolled by some two hundred police officers including one hundred Illinois state police and officers from nearby communities." Hoover was advised in the memo that bureau agents would be on the scene and that the bureau would be kept informed of developments.

Jimi Hendrix

James Marshall Hendrix, a.k.a. Jimi Hendrix, made it into FBI files for seven pages in 1969. The Buffalo office of the FBI cabled the director on June 3, 1969, asking about the arrest record of Jimi Hendrix. By June 10, 1969, the FBI had a memo in their file on Hendrix, and they had given him a file number, 829 158 D, with respect to his arrest record. Hendrix had been busted on May 2, 1961, by the Seattle, Washington, police for taking a car without the owner's permission. His second arrest was four days later in Seattle on May 6, 1961, for taking and riding a motor vehicle without the owner's permission. His final arrest on the 1969 FBI memo was May 3, 1969, by the Toronto Metropolitan Police for illegal possession of narcotics. The memo went on to note that Hendrix was born November 27, 1942, in Seattle, and in 1969 he lived at 27 East 37th Street in New York, N.Y. His occupation was listed as "Musician."

Jim Morrison

Morrison finished in third place for the honor of most pages devoted to a dead rock star in the FBI files. Some ninety-six pages were reviewed by the FBI and five pages were withheld in their entirety. About seventy-six pages of the Morrison file deal with his alleged crimes aboard Continental airlines on a flight from Los Angeles to Phoenix on November 11, 1969—"assault" and "interfering with flight crew." The file also has twelve pages relating to the infamous "Miami exposure incident" of March 1969.

With respect to the Continental airlines flight, the FBI files have numerous eyewitness reports about the alleged behavior of

Morrison and another person. They were said to have created a disturbance by "loud, obscene talk," interfered with instructions on the use of oxygen masks, and kept their feet in the aisle to trip flight attendants. It was alleged that they threw ice from their glasses and "drank and passed" a liquor bottle while in flight. One report said they were "rude" and other reports indicated that they specifically disregarded warnings from head flight attendant and then from the captain of the airplane. Morrison was said to have been walking around and smoking during the time when the "No Smoking" and "Seat Belt" signs were on. The stewardesses were said to have been "frightened" by his behavior.

The file takes the case through the source statements, leads, bureau research, and case disposition. Morrison was described as being a "long haired, hippie type." He was charged with two counts of assault, intimidation, and threatening behavior toward flight attendants. On March 26, 1970, Morrison was found guilty on Count II of indictment and not guilty of Count I. Morrison asked for a new trial on Count II and received it on April 20, 1970. Then on April 20, 1970, he was acquitted of the last charge because the testimony of a government witness in the first trial had been in error. She advised that she had mistakenly identified Morrison as the person who had behaved in a threatening manner; it was the other person that she had meant to identify.

Morrison was arrested ten times from 1963 to 1969. The charges ranged from battery, drunk driving, and driving without a license to lewd and obscene performance, indecent exposure, lascivious behavior, and resisting arrest. When the charges of interference with flight of an aircraft and crime aboard airplane are thrown into his record, one can easily see why Morrison earned the reputation as the "bad boy" of rock.

The Miami incident was described in the FBI file in this manner:

> Jim Morrison, a rock and roll singer, appeared at Dinner Kay Auditorium, Miami, Florida on March 1, 1969. Morrison, a white male, age 25, born in Cocoa Beach, Florida, and once attended Florida State University, reportedly pulled all stops in an effort to provoke chaos among a huge crowd of young people. Morrison's program lasted one hour during which time he sang one song and

for the remainder he grunted, groaned, gyrated and gestured along with inflammatory remarks. He screamed obscenities and exposed himself which resulted in a number of the people on stage being hit and slugged and thrown to the floor.

On such eyewitness reviews as this, Morrison was charged with lewd and lascivious behavior, and he was classified as a "fugitive," under U.S. Code, Title 18, Section 1073. By April 29, 1969, the FBI had been informed that Assistant U.S. Attorney Michael Osman had declined to prosecute Morrison on the charges.

One of the most interesting exchanges in the Morrison file concerns a letter written to J. Edgar Hoover by a private citizen, who expressed his outrage at the current state of rock music. He said, "Certainly, the great majority of decent Americans will applaud any efforts to make record racks and newsstands refrain from peddling such filth." He was referring specifically to the Doors and the Fugs, especially the record "Virgin Fugs." The record was said to be vulgar, repulsive, and most suggestive. After forwarding the record to Robert Mahoney for a decision on whether to prosecute, Hoover replied: "Thank you for your letter of March 20th, with enclosures. I, too, share your concern regarding this type of recording which is being distributed throughout the country and certainly appreciate your bringing it to my attention. It is repulsive to right-thinking people and can have serious effects on our young people."

ELVIS PRESLEY

The Presley file contains eighty-seven pages of extortion and death threats from the 1950s and 1960s, as well as some interesting exchanges between Presley and the FBI. One death threat came to Presley in January 1964 from Huntsville, Alabama. It was addressed to "President Elvis Presley, Memphis S, Tenneesee" [sic] and it read "You will be nest [sic] on my list   1. Elvis Presley 2. Johnny Cash 3. Tommy Moese 4. President LBJ 5. George C. Wallace."

One memo related to Presley's visit to FBI headquarters on December 31, 1970. Presley, it seemed, felt J. Edgar Hoover was one of the greatest living Americans and wanted to meet him when he toured FBI headquarters. The FBI responded that Elvis would get a tour of the headquarters but the director would be unable to see him. A memo entered into Presley's file on January 4, 1971, describes the visit. According to the account, Presley offered his services to the FBI as an undercover, confidential informant. Moreover, he attacked drug use and blamed the Beatles for the problems that America was having with its young people (see figure 10.1).

Given what is now known about Presley's bizarre life style and his use of a whole host of drugs, it is interesting to observe how Presley turned on the "good old boy" Southern charm for the agency.

Fig. 10.1
Memo.

UNITED STATES G ERNMENT

Memorandum

TO   Mr. Bishop   DATE: 1-4-71

FROM   M. A. Jones

SUBJECT: ELVIS PRESLEY
WILLIAM N. MORRIS
FORMER SHERIFF, SHELBY COUNTY, TENNESSEE
BUREAU TOUR 12-31-70

       Presley and Morris and six individuals who provide security for Presley visited FBI Headquarters and were afforded a very special tour of our facilities in accordance with plans approved by the Director.

       Regrets were expressed to Presley and his party in connection with their request to meet the Director. Presley indicated that he has long been an admirer of Mr. Hoover, and has read material prepared by the Director including "Masters of Deceit," "A Study of Communism" as well as "J. Edgar Hoover on Communism." Presley noted that in his opinion no one has ever done as much for his country as has Mr. Hoover, and that he, Presley, considers the Director the "greatest living American." He also spoke most favorably of the Bureau.

       Despite his rather bizarre personal appearance, Presley seemed a sincere, serious minded individual who expressed concern over some of the problems confronting our country, particularly those involving young people. In this regard, in private comments made following his tour, he indicated that he, Presley, is the "living proof that America is the land of opportunity" since he rose from truck driver to prominent entertainer almost overnight. He said that he spends as much time as his schedule permits informally talking to young people and discussing what they consider to be their problems with them. Presley stated that his long hair and unusual apparel were merely tools of his trade and afforded him access to and rapport with many people particularly on college campuses who considered themselves "anti-establishment." Presley said that while he has a limited education, he has been able to command a certain amount of respect and attention from this segment of the population and in an informal way point out the errors of their ways. He advised that he does not consider himself

Enclosure   1-4-71   RLC-79
1 - Mr. Sullivan - Enclosure   1 - Miss Gandy - Enclosure
1 - Mr. Bishop - Enclosure   1 - Miss Holmes - Enclosure
1 - C. D. Brennan - Enclosure   1 - M. A. Jones - Enclosure
GTQ:dkg (9)   (CONTINUED - OVER)

      5 5 JAN 3 1970

(*Fig. 10.1 continued*)

M. A. Jones to Bishop Memo
RE: ELVIS PRESLEY

competent to address large groups but much rather prefers small gatherings in community centers and the like, where he makes himself accessible for talks and discussions regarding the evils of narcotics and other problems of concern to teenagers and other young people.

Following their tour, Presley privately advised that he has volunteered his services to the President in connection with the narcotics problem and that Mr. Nixon had responded by furnishing him an Agent's badge of the Bureau of Narcotics and Dangerous Drugs. Presley was carrying this badge in his pocket and displayed it.

Presley advised that he wished the Director to be aware that he, Presley, from time to time is approached by individuals and groups in and outside of the entertainment business whose motives and goals he is convinced are not in the best interests of this country and who seek to have him to lend his name to their questionable activities. In this regard, he volunteered to make such information available to the Bureau on a confidential basis whenever it came to his attention. He further indicated that he wanted the Director to know that should the Bureau ever have any need of his services in any way that he would be delighted to be of assistance.

Presley indicated that he is of the opinion that the Beatles laid the groundwork for many of the problems we are having with young people by their filthy unkempt appearances and suggestive music while entertaining in this country during the early and middle 1960's. He advised that the Smothers Brothers, Jane Fonda, and other persons in the entertainment industry of their ilk have a lot to answer for in the hereafter for the way they have poisoned young minds by disparaging the United States in their public statements and unsavory activities.

Presley advised that he resides at 3764 Highway 51, South, Memphis, Tennessee, but that he spends a substantial portion of his time in the Beverly Hills, California - Las Vegas, Nevada, areas fulfilling motion picture assignments and singing commitments.

He noted that he can be contacted anytime through his Memphis address and that because of problems he has had with people tampering with his mail, such correspondence should be addressed to him under the pseudonym, Colonel Jon Burrows

- 2 -

CONTINUED - OVER

151

(Fig. 10.1 continued)

M. A. Jones to Bishop Memo
RE: ELVIS PRESLEY

It should be here noted following their tour and prior to their departure from the building, Mr. Morris indicated that Presley had been recently selected by the Junior Chamber of Commerce as one of the "ten outstanding men" in the United States and that of these ten in a ceremony to be held in Memphis sometime in January, 1971, Presley would be named as the "most outstanding" of the ten. According to Morris, similar recognition was afforded President Nixon some 25 years ago and the late President Kennedy was also a recipient of this award.

Morris observed that he has known Presley for many years, that despite his manner of dress, he is a sober, clean minded young man who is good to his family and his friends and who is very well regarded by all, including the law enforcement community in the Memphis, Tennessee, area where he was raised and still resides.

Presley, Morris, and their party expressed appreciation for the courtesies extended them.

OBSERVATION:

Presley did give the impression of being a sincere, young man who is conscious of the many problems confronting this country. In view of his unique position in the entertainment business, his favorable comments concerning the Director and the Bureau, and his offer to be of assistance as well as the fact that he has been recognized by the Junior Chamber of Commerce and the President, it is felt that a letter from the Director would be in order.

RECOMMENDATION:

That the attached letter to Presley be approved and sent.

- 3 -

152

11/The Politics of Rock Music

ROCK MUSIC IS ONE OF the largest entertainment industries along with films, professional sports, and Broadway shows. Rock music is everywhere—in the supermarket, selling products on radio and TV, marketing political candidates at rallies. Rock is used for Broadway plays and for motion picture soundtracks and it plays an important role in many television comedies and dramas. Rock artists appear regularly on television variety shows. Rock music sounds fill parks and concert halls in the 1980s. Moreover rock music is big corporation business in America and around the globe. As David DeVoss has noted: "Over fifty U.S. rock artists annually earn from $2 million to $6 million. At last count, 35 artists and 15 additional groups make from three to seven times more than America's highest paid business executive, Harold Geneen, chief executive officer of ITT."[1]

Rock reaches a vast audience, with some people immersing themselves in the music up to twenty-five hours a week. What, if anything, has rock music been communicating, and to whom is it communicating?

On the whole, as this book has argued, rock music has not been very political. A content analysis of the lyrics of popular songs can reveal that a tiny percentage of rock songs state some kind of political or social message. Most rock songs deal with the classic themes of boy-girl relationships, adolescence, and having a good time. It is a rare rock artist who consistently gives out political messages. Moreover, these political messages do not always have an immediate effect upon the listener. Media tends to reinforce previously held dispositions in most people, and if a contradictory message creates dissonance, the listener can usually block this out through selective perception and selective retention.

Rock songs can have an effect on some people, however, when they concern issues in which the listeners have no opinion, where the songs add completely new information. The cumulative effect of hearing the same rock song or the same basic subject, over and over for a period of months or years, is still uncertain. Yet it does seem to be true that a one-time exposure to a rock song does not affect a listener so much that he or she does whatever the song says to do. The only documented cases of this effect can be seen with unstable individuals who "hear" things in songs that other people do not hear, or interpret the songs in ways that clearly were not intended by the recording artist. For example, Charles Manson thought the Beatles' song "Helter Skelter" was telling him that the time was ripe to carry on an all-out race war in America by perpetuating a series of brutal murders.

Yet given this inability of rock music to change a listener's political and social attitudes, some rock stars are more political and socially conscious than others. Perhaps the "golden era" of political rock music came during the period 1967 to 1971. Certain rock artists were closely tied to the antiwar movement. Some of these were discussed in chapter 9. Other rock groups and artists contributed as well. Among the great antiwar rock groups during this period were Jefferson Airplane and Country Joe and the Fish.

The Airplane had always been the critics' choice during the late 1960s. This spot would be challenged by the Grateful Dead and then by the Allman Brothers Band during the years 1969 to

1971. The Jefferson Airplane included politicos like Grace Slick and Paul Kantner. In 1969 the Airplane released its most important political album, *Volunteers*, which became a classic within the antiwar and student movement. Two songs, "We Can Be Together" and "Volunteers," provided the radical politics for the album, for they were about the "revolution" in the streets.

Grace Slick, one of the most talented women in rock, was assured a place in rock history with "Somebody to Love" and "White Rabbit." For political rockers, a great moment during the antiwar period of 1969 was when Slick sang, "We Can Be Together." Later, the Airplane would split up into the more political Jefferson Starship and the more musical Hot Tuna. Perhaps the Starship's most political album was the Kantner-inspired *Blows Against the Empire.*

Country Joe McDonald and the Fish wrote some of the best antiwar songs of the 1960s. In "Superbird," the Fish sang a parody about Lyndon Baines Johnson. The all-time Country Joe and the Fish classic was, of course, "I Feel Like I'm Fixin' to Die Rag," a humorous song that came at a time when "draft call" and "military build-up" were still code words of the day. Country Joe loved to give his "Fish" cheer before the song, a song that told of the stupidity, immorality, and uselessness of the U.S. involvement in Vietnam. The song is forever captured in the movie documentary of the Woodstock rock festival. Country Joe McDonald went on to pursue a solo career in the 1970s, retaining his strong political conscience while some of his peers in the rock business left theirs behind.

Other rock artists contributed antiwar songs during the golden era of political rock. Jimi Hendrix's electric guitar version of "Star Spangled Banner," complete with bombs bursting in air, was a radically different, highly political rendition of the national anthem. Black artists like Edwin Starr sang "War" and Freda Payne sang "Bring the Boys Home" to contribute to the growing volume of antiwar songs.

While the film industry would not cover the Vietnam war until the late 1970s with films like *Deerhunter, Coming Home*, and *Apocalypse Now*, the rock industry had a number of stars who contributed significant antiwar statements at a time when it really counted, when the Vietnam war was still going on.

Donovan sang Buffy Sainte Marie's "Universal Soldier" and Mick Softly's "The War Drags On" as early as 1965. In "The War Drags On," Softly laments the fact that the Vietnam war appears to be never ending. Little did he know that this song would apply to U.S. involvement until January 1973.

The Doors, with their lead singer Jim Morrison, contributed the "Unknown Soldier," in which Morrison announced the end of the war. Eric Burdon, former lead singer of the Animals, sang "Sky Pilot" during this golden era of political rock. "Sky Pilot" was a song addressed to all the military pilots who participated in the various bombings in Laos, Cambodia, and North and South Vietnam. Burdon questioned how these pilots could continue to kill people and still be immune from the horror of war.

Frank Zappa and the Mothers of Invention were one of the most socially and politically relevant groups of the late 1960s and early 1970s. This group provided their share of anti-establishment tunes. Zappa had a fine sense of political humor, but unfortunately his group's messages did not reach a large audience since the Mothers of Invention was an "underground" band. Many times their subtle messages were too complex for mass audiences, but their cult following looked upon the Mothers as one of the greatest rock acts ever assembled.

Steppenwolf, with lead singer John Kay, did an entire rock album aimed at the "monster" (the United States). Creedence Clearwater Revival contributed the working-class, beer drinking, antiwar rocker "Fortunate Son." The song questioned a double standard in America, where the poor boys went off to fight and the rich stayed at home. The song was a concise critique of the military-industrial complex, denouncing favoritism for the sons of senators, millionaires, and military men.

The various contributions of rock stars to the antiwar movement cannot be easily measured. Some Top 40 acts would have one political song out of eleven on an album and get credit for being "political." Yet this emergence of politicized rock in the years 1967 to 1971 helped create three distinct cultures within the so-called youth movement: the rock culture, the radical political culture, and the dope culture. Though they were distinct cultures, they intermingled.

The rock culture could be observed in the growing rock industry, the increase in album sales, the tremendous fan worship, and the phenomenon of groupies. This was an era of supergroups such as Blind Faith and Crosby, Stills, Nash, and Young and a time when extraordinary rock talents died at the height of their careers—Janis Joplin, Jimi Hendrix, Brian Jones, Jim Morrison, and Duane Allman. Giant rock festivals and small theater shows at the Fillmore East and the Fillmore West took place. And it was an era when a small rock magazine called *Rolling Stone*, under the direction of Jann Wenner, developed into the bible of rock journalism. It was easy for masses of young people to participate in the rock culture during those years. One just selected some favorite groups, bought their recorded products, attended concerts, and became a "fan."

The dope culture also spread during the years 1967-1971. Timothy Leary advocated a sense of community that could come from the common experience of LSD. Ken Kesey, the Grateful Dead, and a host of psychedelic rockers seemed to agree. There were other drugs to be purchased easily and at reasonable prices, including marijuana, hashish, uppers and downers, mescaline, and cocaine. Corporations picked up on various drug themes and jargon and incorporated them into their advertisements. Hip comedians made reference to drug use. If rock became big business in America during this period, then "recreational" drugs for the white middle class became a big and profitable underground business.

The radical political culture tried to gain recruits from the rock and dope cultures, but converts were not easy to come by. Rock music was too entertaining to present a serious indictment of American society, and, moreover, the rock culture was one that inherently relied on capitalistic measures of success in the form of who sold the most records, what position the album had on *Billboard* charts, and how many fans attended a concert; it also depended on the capitalistic technology that was needed to make a record. It was difficult for a singer to be part of a truly radical political culture and not suffer economically. The dope culture's adherents were so stoned that it was difficult for the radical political culture to attract them as converts; serious political thought drastically decreases when one is using a drug for pleasure.

In this cultural milieu, there were still those who persisted in trying to bring the distinct and even exclusive cultures together. These included hippies and yippies, politicians, commentators in *Time, Life, Newsweek,* and *Rolling Stone,* and writers like Charles Reich. The idea was that all three cultures were truly one and that they formed a new American "revolution" in terms of economic, political, religious, and social values. The simplicity of that argument attracted ever more opinion leaders and analysts. Young people were going to save America from racial injustice, the war in Vietnam, and the evils of corporate capitalism by smoking a lot of dope, buying the new album by Jefferson Airplane, and reciting rhetoric from Jerry Rubin or Abbie Hoffman, or so it seemed. Few at the time realized how different each of those cultures really was.

The various "culture freaks" from each of the distinct camps disagreed over the role of rock music. For some, rock music was the mechanism that would help form a new, alternative culture that would go "back to the land," live communally, "do dope," and try new sexual relationships while ignoring the establishment. The radical political culture thought rock music should be used as an organizing tool to enlist militant activists who would fight repression in all forms, the war, the military, capitalism, environmental destroyers, sexism, and large corporations. For others, rock music was to be used for lighting up, boogying, making love, and relieving boredom.

The radical political culture freaks liked only a few serious artists such as Phil Ochs and Joan Baez. They rejected the rock culture because it allowed people to escape serious political thinking and because the rock culture stars had become rich like other American capitalists. Rock stars were perceived by the radical political culture as artists who had the power to change society but who opted to sell out the "revolution."

ROCK AND REVOLUTION

Many thought that rock music could be a tool for a real revolution in America. Jim Morrison said: "Erotic politicians, that's what we are. We're interested in anything about revolt, disorder, chaos and activity that appears to have no meaning."[2]

For some, rock would create a social revolution in consciousness. In this spirit, Country Joe McDonald observed, "The
most revolutionary thing you can do in this country is change
your mind."[3]

Two rock groups in particular started out specifically to be
"rock and revolution" groups, but only one made it commercially. These groups were the MC5 and Chicago. The MC5 were
managed by White Panther John Sinclair. They had their own
brand of hard-driving rock that "kicked out the jams," but they
failed to gain a mass audience. As rock critic Ben Fong-Torres
noted, "They wanted to be bigger than the Beatles; he [John
Sinclair] wanted them to be bigger than Mao."[4]

MC5 was part of the Ann Arbor (Michigan) politico-social
scene, and their audiences were mostly composed of "street people" and "freaks." In the early 1970s, after Sinclair was busted
for marijuana possession, the group began having serious problems. Their new manager, rock critic Jon Landau, wanted them
to drop all their political rhetoric and become a cultural force
within the rock industry. Yet the band was caught in a dilemma.
If they compromised their political positions so they could be
commerically successful, then they would lose their original
following. The fact that their best album sold only 100,000 copies
did the MC5 in. Though some rock critics thought they were a
new, great force in music, the mass audience had problems with
rock and revolution. The MC5 quickly became the "George
McGovern" of political rock and faded away.

The rock group Chicago, which was originally called Chicago
Transit Authority or CTA, became one of the most commercially
successful groups ever to record. Even though Chicago started
out as a "rock and revolution" band, it was never really clear
whether the group was politically active early on because producer James William Guercio thought activism would sell or
because they were sincere. Chicago had a big rock-jazz band
sound, replete with horns, that sold more than forty million
albums for the group in 1974. For the mass rock audience,
Chicago was clearly doing something right. Yet after their first
two albums, the politics of the group began to disappear.

Chicago's first album contained tributes to the Chicago
anti-war demonstrations at the Chicago Democratic national
convention in 1968, including some live recordings of the street

confrontations between police and demonstrators in a song called "Liberation." The second Chicago album was dedicated to "the people of the revolution...and the revolution in all its forms." For many activists it was absurd for Chicago to sing about revolution when they were making millions of dollars on each album and not filtering the money back into the movement. In effect, Chicago profited from the movement ethos. Later, in 1972, to show how revolutionary they had become, the group started pushing voter registration for young people. They supported George McGovern for the presidency and did some work to raise money for him. This was hardly the radical critique of society that some people thought Chicago had promised.

McGovern's defeat in 1972 ended the group's participation in politics, except for a post-Watergate tune about the need for Harry Truman to return to the presidency. Chicago retired on their beautiful Caribou ranch in Colorado for the rest of the 1970s, making albums and millions of dollars. One way to get back to the land, they found, was to buy it! Lead singer Robert Lamm summed up his political involvement in the 1970s: "At the time 1972 I really gave a shit, but I don't anymore. If McGovern could lose by that margin, then I and everybody I know must be nothing."[5]

Perhaps the incident that best portrayed the problems of combining rock and revolution in the United States came when Peter Townshend of the Who hit Abbie Hoffman over the head with his guitar at Woodstock in 1969. Hoffman wanted to turn the Woodstock Nation on to some radical political ideas during the Who's set, and Townshend indicated where his priorities were by bashing away at Hoffman. Later Townshend would write one of his best songs, "Won't Get Fooled Again," that warned people not to follow the new revolutionary leaders and the rhetoric of the movement because everyone got fooled by those leaders and gurus in the 1960s. Townshend hoped that people would not get fooled again. Ironically, Townshend became a spiritual rock guru for many people in the 1970s, precisely the sort of thing that he had spoken out against in the early 1970s and in his 1960s rock opera *Tommy*.

By most accounts, the experience of rock and revolution in the United States was a failure. Rock failed to gain converts for the so-called revolution and the revolution "in all its forms" did not seem to be scoring the kinds of successes that a revolution needs to sustain itself.

POLITICAL ROCK IN THE MID 1970S: AFTER THE FALL

The demise of political rock came after the May Day demonstrations in Washington, D.C., in 1971, and this reflected an end to an era of protest. Rock music was not politicized during the great commercial successes of the rock industry in the so-called "me decade" of the 1970s.

Rock music continued to branch out in new directions—theatrical rock, glitter rock, black superstar pop rock, disco, jazz, country, southern rock, art rock, women's rock, and LA rock, to name a few. The Watergate crisis should have been covered in many rock songs; instead, there was almost no response by rock poets. Lynyrd Skynyrd captured this feeling in "Sweet Home Alabama" (1974) when listeners were asked if Watergate bothered them, the implication being that it clearly didn't bother the band. Only such popular acts as Neil Young and Arlo Guthrie showed any understanding of the Watergate affair in their songs.

Post-Watergate rock in the 1970s lacked excitement for the most part. Rock concerts had become so ritualized that few people went to them to actually listen to the music, rather they went "to make the scene." Matches were ignited at the right time to call for encores, even if the groups were performing their songs in poor fashion. Rock developed into a "monster out of control" in the 1970s as the prices of concerts and albums more than kept pace with inflation. For many acts, artistry vanished; money was the only name of the game. Companies and artists searched for "monster" albums like *Peter Frampton Comes Alive*, Fleetwood Mac's *Rumours*, the soundtrack of *Saturday Night Fever*, or Carole King's *Tapestry*. The institutionalization of rock music came about in the 1970s as rock developed a set of standard operating procedures within popular culture. The key idea for the artist was to be "safe" and not to take chances. Yet, as Jon Landau has observed about rock, "It's too late to stop now!"[6]

The 1970s saw the glitter-rock culture, which owed a debt to the gay liberation movement of the early 1970s and the influences of Mick Jagger and Ray Davies (Kinks) in the 1960s. David Bowie, Alice Cooper, the New York Dolls, and a host of other glitter rockers made ambisexual poses on stage complete with make-up and feminine fashions. As rock philosopher Frank Zappa once said, "We're only in it for the money!"

Another trend in the 1970s saw the black artist finally getting some big bucks by taking to the middle-of-the-road, middle-class pop market. Stevie Wonder, Al Green, the Commodores, Marvin Gaye, and Michael Jackson all made significant sales to the young pop-rock masses. In some circles, Stevie Wonder was recognized as the pop artist of the 1970s. Sly and the Family Stone and Jimi Hendrix had been influential with white audiences from 1967 to 1971, but Wonder surpassed their influence in the 1970s. Black artists had been denied big profits in rock music for many years, though white artists often used black trends to make a profit. Finally, with the success of disco in the mid-1970s, many more black artists were able to share some of the rock 'n' roll money. This helped in some small way to reverse a trend that Immamu Amiri Baraka (LeRoi Jones) had noted about white rockers: they stole from blacks and kept all the money.[7]

The Byrds, Bob Dylan, and Neil Young started a down-home, back-to-nature, plain shirt, heart-of-gold, and cabin-in-Utah brand of rock in the late 1960s and early 1970s. In the remaining years of the 1970s, Jackson Browne, James Taylor, and Neil Young continued the tradition. Other country rock groups, like the Eagles, became superstars with their brand of Los Angeles-country-desert rock. Country rock branched out into southern rock, led by the Allman Brothers Band, the Marshall Tucker Band, Lynyrd Skynyrd, and the Charlie Daniels Band. The mountain minstrel was represented in the pop field by John Denver. The country rock explosion also allowed real country-and-western artists to become stars in the world of rockdom—Waylon Jennings, Willie Nelson, and Dolly Parton. And washed-up rock acts like Kenny Rogers crossed over into the field of country music to score amazing successes.

The infusion of great jazz artists into the rock market also took place in the 1970s with artists like Herbie Hancock, Miles Davis, John McLaughlin, Billy Cobham, and Chick Corea leading the way. Young record buyers were inspired to go back and pick up on earlier jazz greats like Charlie Parker, Pharoah Sanders, John Coltrane, Ornette Coleman, and Thelonious Monk.

The female rock singer finally had her day in the 1970s, even though rock music essentially was still a sexist institution. Joni Mitchell, Carole King, Carly Simon, Bonnie Raitt, Bette Midler, and particularly Linda Ronstadt sold many records and received critical acclaim. In the 1960s, other than the black soul singers and the "girl groups," women in rock had been limited to Grace Slick and Janis Joplin. The 1970s saw women taking an independent role and scoring as solo acts. Other acts like Heart, led by Nancy and Ann Wilson, and Pat Benatar scored impressive hits in the 1970s. Middle-of-the-road female pop singers like Olivia Newton-John, Marie Osmond, Ann Murray, Karen Carpenter, and Helen Reddy sold records in the rock market also.

Perhaps the most significant trend of the middle 1970s in rock was the tremendous popularity of disco. Disco broke into the mainstream with songs by Donna Summer, Gloria Gaynor, the Bee Gees, and the Village People. Summer emerged as the queen of disco, and later crossed over into the rock and soul market. Disco created an alternative culture to the remnants of the rock and dope cultures of the 1960s. The disco culture stressed whirling dance lights, fashionable designer jeans, and monotonous, computerized, loud synthetic music that did not require the listener to think at all.

But of all these trends, none except the punk rock/new wave movement could be considered political. Mostly they reflected a dissatisfaction with rock and politics and represented a retreat from sociopolitical stances of the 1960s and 1970s. Only a few rock artists had been political from 1967 to 1971, and as these artists began their retreat in the "me decade" of introspection and self-improvement, the political content of rock turned into an apathetic stance. The songs of the 1970s tended to be about personal love experiences, or about nature, or about deep and personal emotions.

There was no great coverage by rock songwriters of the U.S. government's continuation of the Vietnam war well past 1971 until 1973, nor of the CIA's involvement in the overthrow of Chilean president Salvador Allende, except, of course, for the outrage shown by Phil Ochs and Arlo Guthrie. There were no popular rock acts that tried to get across political messages about great political problems in the 1970s such as the CIA-FBI revelations, the problems of world food distribution and hunger, human rights violations, and domination by multinational corporations. Instead the messages reflected a return to the traditional themes of rock as covered by two of the biggest superstars of the 1970s, Elton John and Bruce Springsteen. John covered teenage love, feelings, and good times, while Springsteen, showing some lower-middle-class economic resentment for life in America, sang about cars, cruising, racing, teenage girls, early romances, backseat love, teenage fantasies, and walking down the street with his friends.

Except for an occasional Jackson Browne or Neil Young tune about the lost idealism of the "movement" or a John Denver ecology song or a Stevie Wonder antiracism song, political themes in rock music were almost nonexistent up to the punk rock/new wave explosion of the late 1970s.

Rock has its social relevancy. The Gallup Youth Survey in 1977 captured the sad state of rock in music by surveying 1,069 teenagers in a random national sample. The top twenty individuals and groups among U.S. teenagers were ranked as follows[8]:

1. Kiss	11. Barry Manilow
2. Eagles	12. Elton John
3. Beatles	13. Beach Boys
4. Led Zeppelin	14. Stevie Wonder
5. Boston	15. Barbra Streisand
6. Chicago	16. Jacksons
7. Aerosmith	17. Bee Gees
8. Peter Frampton	18. Rolling Stones
9. Earth, Wind and Fire	19. Wings
10. K.C. and the Sunshine Band	20. John Denver

One fan reported about Kiss: "They're a unique group; they do what they feel on the stage and show you a good time. They paint their bodies and shoot off rockets and things like that."[9] An Eagles fan observed about his favorite group: "They're easy listening compared to a lot of the rock you hear. Their music is very relaxing and just flows. They have a clear, nice-sounding tone."[10]

Teenage America's top twenty artists of 1977 clearly revealed the state of political rock. There was not a true political rocker among them. During the 1976 presidential campaign candidate for president Jimmy Carter quoted Bob Dylan and announced his love for Southern rock music. In 1974 during a Georgia Law Day speech in Athens, Carter said: "One of the sources for my understanding about the proper application of justice and the system of equity is from reading Reinhold Niebuhr...the other source of my understanding about what's right and wrong in this society is from a friend of mine, a poet named Bob Dylan. After listening to his records about 'The Ballad of Hattie Carol,' and 'Like a Rolling Stone,' and 'The Times They Are a-Changing,' I've learned to appreciate the dynamism of change in modern society."[11] Later on the campaign trail he would talk about rock stars in these terms: "In present music, I think, strangely enough, my affinity for music has shifted from classical music to a much more contemporary music. Bob Dylan is a good friend of mine. I like Paul Simon. I like the Marshall Tucker Band. I like Gregg Allman and the Allman Brothers. They're my friends. They raise money for me. I look toward them almost as though they were my own children."[12]

When presidential candidates quote rock stars and proclaim them to be their friends, it becomes quite clear that rock is no longer a threatening force to the elites. Rock had grown lazy and tame in all of its overblown opulence; it was hardly on the cutting edge of societal change. Rock stars had to pay for their homes on the West Coast, the drugs, the limousines, and the good times. American popular culture easily absorbed the rock star into its class structure.

ROCK AND SOCIAL ACTION

Though the 1970s saw the end of politics in rock music lyrics, that period continued the trend of the 1960s of rock performers doing benefits for a cause. Folksingers like Arlo Guthrie, Phil Ochs, and Joan Baez found a small audience within rock for their political messages in the 1960s and early 1970s. These entertainers built up an impressive record of playing political and social benefits to show that they really did care. Guthrie's music had important implications for the spread of draft resistance when his *Alice's Restaurant* became a best-selling song, album, and motion picture. Guthrie's heritage from his populist folk-singing father, Woody Guthrie, guided him in his statements against war, racism, the FBI misuse of government power, Watergate, Nixon, and Agnew. Moreover, Guthrie did political benefits to back Chilean freedom fighters, and he cut a song in tribute to Chilean poet Victor Jara, who was brutally murdered by a military junta in Chile that was backed by the U.S. government.

Phil Ochs was one of the most consistent political folksingers in the 1960s, and he retained his political conscience long after his friend Bob Dylan gave it up to become a rock star. In the 1960s, Ochs recorded songs like "Talking Vietnam" and "Talking Cuban Crisis" along with "I Ain't Marching Anymore." He also shared his political ideology on record with "There but for Fortune," "Draft Dodger Rag," "Here's to the State of Mississippi" and "The War Is Over," to name but a few of the many Ochs political statements. The important thing about Phil Ochs, however, was that he did benefits to help the antiwar movement. He also performed at the countergathering for demonstrators at the 1968 Democratic national convention in Chicago. He tried to raise money for the defense of his friend Jerry Rubin and others charged in the Chicago 7 trial. District Judge Julius J. Hoffman refused to allow Ochs to enter his song "I Ain't Marching Anymore" into the trial record.

In 1971, Ochs was one of the few politicos to show up at the May Day demonstrations to entertain at a rock concert. In 1974, Ochs helped organize a tribute to Salvador Allende, the assassinated leader of Chile, and he got Bob Dylan to perform at Madison Square Garden.[13] His last major rally was a Central Park concert to celebrate the conclusion of the Vietnam war on May 11, 1975. Tragically, Ochs was unable to deal with a host of personal problems, the decline of radical politics, and the failure of his career in the nonpolitical 1970s, and took his own life on April 9, 1976.

Joan Baez became an important popular-culture figure in the late 1960s because she remained committed to her "radical" belief in nonviolent civil disobedience as a tool of social change.

In the early 1960s she had been the sweetheart of the folk set as she sang songs about racial injustice and urged an end to war. She and Bob Dylan were often paired by her fans as the queen and king of folk protest. But as the 1960s progressed, Baez became a nonviolent social activist. She really believed in the themes that she had been singing about almost a decade earlier. She opposed nationalism and violence of any kind. She spoke out against the war in Vietnam and participated in the mass marches on Washington, D.C., while her friend Bob Dylan remained silent. She worked to establish centers for the study of nonviolence and to aid draft resisters. She worked for prison reform when her husband, draft resister David Harris, was sent to prison. She made the rounds on the talk shows in the late 1960s and early 1970s, saying those radical things that had to be said to Americans, and she performed this role with great dignity.

In short, during the intense antiwar period of 1967-1971, Joan Baez along with John Lennon was probably the most important, consistent, radical, and influential politico from the music industry. She was one of the few who did more than sing about injustice. She acted. Few performers can make such a claim.

Though Guthrie, Ochs, and particularly Baez established the pattern of social action in the 1960s and early 1970s, other performers continued to raise money for various political and social causes in the mid and late 1970s. George Harrison gave a concert in 1971 to raise funds for starving refugees in Bangladesh. He convinced Bob Dylan, Eric Clapton, Ringo Starr, Leon Russell, Ravi Shankar, Billy Preston, Klaus Voorman, and others to play the Madison Square Garden benefit. The concert raised $243,418 for the United Nations Children's Fund for Relief to Refugee Children of Bangladesh. The check was made out on August 12, 1971, yet there is still a question about whether the money ever reached Bangladesh refugees. Other concerts were performed during the 1970s for various causes, such as prison reform, Bay Area charities, the Vietnam boat people, the Cambodian refugees, world hunger, defense fund for Rubin "Hurricane" Carter, and to fight racism.

Singer-songwriter Harry Chapin established a remarkable record during the 1970s by performing at benefits for various causes, in particular, the elimination of world hunger. In fact,

Chapin became a full-fledged food activist and lobbyist as he testified before congressional hearings. By 1978, Chapin and others had put enough pressures on the appropriate centers in Washington to get a joint congressional resolution calling for the establishment of a Presidential Commission on Domestic and International Hunger and Malnutrition.[14] Since 1973, Chapin raised an average of $500,000 a year for the cause of world hunger, and by all accounts, this money reached agencies that could distribute food in an effective way. In 1977 in Detroit, Chapin convinced John Denver, James Taylor, and Gordon Lightfoot to join him for a concert to combat world hunger. Throughout the 1970s he got other friends in the music business to donate time and effort for the cause. For Chapin that cause remained a central focus in his activities until the tragic automobile accident that claimed his life in 1981. As consumer activist Ralph Nader observed about Chapin's dedication: "I've never seen an example of an entertainer who dedicated so many hours or so much imagination to a civic cause. A lot of them go to soirees, a lot of them give lip service, but the duration of Harry's commitment is unprecedented. Congress has seen a lot of guys come here for certain causes, but after a few days or a few hours, they're gone. Harry's committed to this issue on a permanent basis."[15]

Probably the most exciting use of rock for a social cause came with the series of rock concerts and one public rally in September 1979 in New York City sponsored by Musicians United for Safe Energy, or MUSE. The "No Nukes" concerts were the idea of the founders of MUSE, John Hall, Jackson Browne, Bonnie Raitt, Graham Nash, and four antinuclear activists, Sam Lovejoy, Howard Kohn, Tom Campbell and David Fenton.[16] John Hall had written and performed an antinuclear power song called "Power." The other rock stars had been in opposition to nuclear power since the early and mid 1970s, specifically the proposed nuclear power plant in California at Diablo Canyon. Jackson Browne had long donated the sale of concert T-shirts to the antinuclear power movement, but the "No Nukes" concert was the first time that a rock concert was put on in order to raise money for antinuke groups.

The "No Nukes" concerts were extraordinarily successful in raising money through the sale of tickets, a record album, and a movie about the concerts in Madison Square Garden. Among the rock stars that performed during the concert series were Bruce Springsteen, the Doobie Brothers, James Taylor, David Crosby, Stephen Stills, Carly Simon, Jesse Colin Young, and Nicolette Larson along with earlier rock activists like Bonnie Raitt, John Hall, Graham Nash, and Jackson Browne. Superstar Bruce Springsteen agreed to play only after learning that none of the money would go to any specific politicians, and when Springsteen played on the bill, the concerts were assured of having a large East Coast attendance.

The "No Nukes" concerts received adequate media coverage and the rally was well attended. Extraordinary amounts of money were made for the antinuclear cause, but compared to the amount of money the oil corporations, utilities, and the nuclear industry have, the "No Nukes" money was minimal at best. The concerts helped to give the antinuclear-power movement a shot in the arm in the late 1970s as some of the notoriety from the events at Three Mile Island began to fade from the national consciousness.

The concerts, although unable to stop nuclear power, at least helped gain money and publicity for the cause. They resparked the idea that rock music could be used for social change. Even though most people who attended the Madison Square Garden concerts were decidedly apolitical and apathetic about nuclear power, the fans came to see and hear their favorite rock stars and thereby helped to raise money for a cause. If Jackson Browne symbolized the consciousness of some young rock fans with his "Before the Deluge," then Springsteen symbolized the majority spirit among rock fans by doing his Mitch Ryder and the Detroit Wheels' medley of songs, the message being, "boogie, party, and have a good time."

THE POLITICS OF ROCK IN THE 1980S

Rock music in the 1980s retains its apolitical and apathetic posture toward the world of current events, except for the exciting strand of punk rock/new wave rockers, and a few others like Warren Zevon, Neil Young, Jackson Browne, and veterans from the golden era of political rock.

The punk explosion in the late 1970s grew out of the frustrations of lower-class English kids who were trying to make it economically and socially in a country that had produced Rod Stewart, Elton John, and Paul McCartney. The infamous Sex Pistols, with Johnny Rotten and Sid Vicious, helped ignite the trend in 1977, but the group burned out before they could ride the crest of commercial popularity. Another group, the Clash, was also instrumental in forming the new punk consciousness in England in 1977; by the 1980s, the Clash had become international superstars despite the fact that punkers disdained commercial popularity because it tended to make an artist lose touch with his or her rock 'n' roll roots.

The Clash, with its own brand of leftist, nihilistic politics played with punk rock's minimalistic sensibilities, became the best and most political of the punk rock groups. On the group's first album, called The Clash, the band composed of Joe Strummer, Mick Jones, Paul Simonon, and Nicky Headon perform radical street songs in machine-gun fashion, such as "London's Burning," "Police and Thieves," "White Riot," and "I'm So Bored with the USA."[17] This group certainly was saying something different than "let's disco the night away." In "I'm So Bored with the USA," the Clash condemns the United States as a place where killers worked every day of the week and as a hypocritical country that could best be symbolized by the Watergate tapes.

Other Clash albums continued this trend toward the politicization of punk. Their late-1979 album that ushered in the 1980s was called London Calling. The title track told of an apocalypse coming to the Western world, especially to London. The song was performed with a great sense of urgency, as though it were the final warning before all political systems as we know them would break down. The album describes confrontations with police and authorities and comments on international repression by superpowers in Third World countries. The Clash even returned to the late 1960s by offering a song called "Revolution Rock," only this time it sounded more like the artists really meant it. As Mick Jones once said, "This is a fact—people prefer to dance than to fight wars."[18]

The Clash scored musically and artistically. They gained a following in the United States despite their politics, which many labeled as juvenile, leftist, trivial, or meaningless. The group joined Tom Robinson and others to do benefits for an organization known as Rock Against Racism. The Clash clearly were anti-right wing, anti-fascist, and anti-Nazi in their orientation. As Mick Jones stated: "Any gig we do is Rock Against Racism because we play black music; we're as interested in making sure that the black culture survives as much as that the white culture does. We play their music and hope they'll play ours. We have a common bond with these people."[19]

Later, when Jones was asked if the movement in England of Rock Against Racism was started because Eric Clapton came out in support of English right-wing politician Enoch Powell, who wanted to send England's blacks to Africa, Jones responded: "Eric Clapton is just an old idiot. Who cares? He's got the opinions of a bricklayer, and he plays guitar like it, as well! Don't care how laid-back he is, it's bricklaying politics. Drinking beer up against the bar with the lads. Leave him out of it. He made an idiot out of himself, that's the thing. I don't find that kind of thing admirable in an artist."[20]

In early 1981, the Clash continued their trend of left-wing, political, punk-rock albums with *Sandinista*, which identifies with various left-wing guerrilla movements in the Third World that seek to fight repression. With political tunes like "Ivan Meets GI Joe," "Charlie Don't Surf," "Police on My Back," and "The Leader," to name a few, the Clash once again announced Armageddon. Perhaps the best political number on the three record set, which featured reggae, black rhythms, and old rock riffs, is "Washington Bullets." The Clash detail their historical version of U.S. imperialism and oppression in Latin America and they clearly side with the liberators, the Sandinista. Perhaps the Clash's contribution to rock in the 1980s is the fact that they are one of the few groups willing to politicize their lyrics. The album *Combat Rock* (1982) is an example.

Other punk-rock/new-wave acts that showed a certain amount of political and social consciousness included the Gang of Four, the Bus Boys, Tom Robinson, Talking Heads, and the only superstar to come out of the new wave tradition, Elvis Costello. Elvis Costello and the Attractions mellowed by the 1980s, but some of their late-1970s releases indicated that the prolific songwriter Costello also had some positions with respect to war, mercenaries, and society.

Punk-rock/new-wave is only a small part of the rock scene in the 1980s. The diversity of rock music as seen in the 1970s explosion has continued. No single trend dominates, and political rock music in mainstream rock is still almost nonexistent. Clever Warren Zevon gave away his political stances, as did Jackson Browne and a few others, but rock, with the exception of some punk rockers, mostly continues in an apolitical and apathetic way.

One could predict for the rest of the 1980s that if some political event directly influenced the mass rock audience or if student activism returned on the level of the 1960s to protest, say, a prolonged war in Central America, then rock music artists would cover the topical aspects of the confrontation. Rock acts best as a mirror to reflect what is going on in society. Rarely, if ever, has rock played an important role in changing peoples' political attitudes. If society is apolitical and apathetic about political issues, then rock will reflect this. Moreover, if political rock returns to a fairly profitable status as in the 1960s, then record labels would be willing to put out more politicized albums as a rock fad.

Music does have the power, of course, to mobilize people and create a sense of community as in the reggae music played by Bob Marley and the Wailers and Toot and the Maytals for Rastafarians in Jamaica. Yet in the United States as the rock industry continues to grow and diversify each year, it becomes increasingly difficult to find a style of rock music that all listeners can rally around or a style that can create a sense of community for young people. Perhaps there are no unifying rock heroes left in the 1980s, only many rock millionaires. Or perhaps, as mythological rock hero Jimmy Thudpucker believes, the question of rock heroes is all timing.

Thudpucker, in the rock interview done by his creator Gary Trudeau for *Rolling Stone*, talked about how his fictional song, "I Do Believe," had become one of the most celebrated songs of our times back in 1969. Thudpucker told Trudeau: "It was all timing, man. How was anyone to know that the D.C. Park Police were right near the breaking point. Actually Strawberry Alarm Clock was due to go on before me, but their drummer got caught in traffic. Now if the cat had made it, the band would have gone on, and the cops would have reached critical mass the first time someone hit a high C, and the anthem for a entire generation would have been "Incense and Peppermints." It was all timing, man. I got lucky."[21]

The politics of rock music appears to be all timing.

12/Conclusion

IN THE 1980s, ROCK MUSIC continues on a course that was established in the 1950s and that course is one that provides entertainment, fun, and relief from boredom. It has rarely provided serious political messages that influenced its listeners to change their attitudes or to take up arms.

Rock music has reflected what was going on in society. Thus during times of political unrest, some rock music reflected that political unrest, but rock basically acts as a regime-maintaining institution in that it keeps people from serious political thought. If fans really thought about the political problems of the world—starvation, nuclear holocaust, inadequate government leaders, unemployment, or economic ills—then the political arena would be a much different place. Rock music is a very entertaining opiate.

Rock music allows the fan to escape, to relax, and to dream. It helps conjure up images of a continuous state of adolescent life. It allows thirty- and even forty-year-olds to sing the praises of the teenage existential condition. Ian Drury and the Blockheads described the relationship better than any social scientist, I believe, when they sang about "Sex and Dope and Rock and Roll."

Rock music is the key communicating agent for young Americans in the 1980s. It is on television, records, cassettes, radio, in movies, advertisements, and supermarkets. The average amount of time that rock music invades one's consciousness, whether intentionally or subliminally, is outrageously high. Adolescent males and females rate "listening to music" as their most popular way to relax, to be entertained, and to be relieved from loneliness.[1] One study found that listening to music ranked second only to "going off by myself" as a way to cope, to deal with feelings of anger and hurt.[2]

Rock music reflects racism and sexism in its songs and in its institutional practices, and it reflects conspicuous consumption in the image of rock star life. Rock music has rarely shown a radical political nature because radical politics has rarely been high on popular culture discussion agenda except in the late 1960s and early 1970s.

Most of the political rock songs were not very radical, except for a few John Lennon songs, some songs by the Clash, and a few others. Bob Dylan did not recognize the similarities between rock stars and politicians in a statement in 1965 when he tried to put down all politicians; "They've got a commodity to sell and that commodity is themselves. Politics is just a commercial bandwagon."[3] Yet as Steve Chapple and Reebee Garofalo have shown, "rock 'n' roll is here to pay," and rock music is just one big commodity to sell and nothing else.[4]

In rock culture, few rock politicos have shown the same sincerity and conviction of their political beliefs that folk protest singers Phil Ochs and Joan Baez have in the folk arena.[5] The key problem in the politics of rock music seems to be lack of sincerity and commitment. It is difficult for rock stars who make such high salaries to sing songs about the need to redistribute the wealth or to attack their "capitalist" record companies. The rock world thrives on capitalistic consumption. Rock stars are the new pampered elite—the rich and famous. If artists sing about their own experience, then the 1980s should show a continuation of songs about sex, dope, entertainment, and fun. Few songs will cover poverty, racism, unemployment, and sexism in the 1980s, since these are beyond the experience of most rock stars.

The early 1980s were not kind to the few remaining political rockers who entered the fourth decade of rock. John Lennon was assassinated, reggae-rock politico Bob Marley died, and Harry Chapin, the singer-world hunger activist, died in an automobile accident. This left rock culture with only the politics of Jackson Browne, Bruce Springsteen, and the punk rock/new wave acts to look forward to in the 1980s. Jackson Browne had gone from being an idealistic singer-songwriter in the early 1970s, who sang about the innocence of youth, to a nuclear activist. In 1982, Browne participated in the Diablo Canyon demonstrations, making the national news when he was arrested for criminal trespassing. Moreover, Browne was one of the important stars in the group Musicians United for Safe Energy (MUSE).

Springsteen's politics were important because he was perceived to be the great rocker in the early 1980s. He at times sang about the problems of working-class people and their lack of opportunities in the United States. He also did MUSE concerts, as well as benefits for the forgotten Vietnam veterans. Fans of punk rock/new wave groups had a wide range of politicos from which to choose, including the Maoist group, the Gang of Four, as well as the witty, sarcastic Ray Davies and the Kinks. The Kinks were the only group from the British invasion to become more popular after the punk rock/new wave explosion in the late 1970s. Davies continued to be the best commentator in songs about societal foibles. Yet the main thrust of punk rock/new wave politics came from groups like the Clash. During the summer of 1981, riots broke out in many major English cities between young people and authorities. The violence and the climate for riots among young, unemployed whites and blacks in England had been forecast in various songs, such as the Sex Pistols' "Anarchy in U.K." (1976) and the Clash's "White Riot" (1977). It was not so much a case of life imitating art as it was art (rock music) accurately reflecting the tensions among a group of alienated people in British society.

Thus, in order to understand the state of the politics of rock music, it is important to look at the political attitudes of the fans of Jackson Browne, Bruce Springsteen, and punk rock/new wave acts. The rankings in figures 12.1, 12.2, and 12.3 show how fans of each musical style related to political symbols when asked to rank terms. Fans were asked to give party identification, political ideology, and other background details. Then they were asked to rank fifty or so political terms by assigning scores of positive 2, positive 1, zero, negative 1, or negative 2. The results indicate that fans of these three styles of music do not have radical political feelings.

Though these rock fans were surveyed at a private Jesuit institution, the results show that a person's favorite rock star does not have a great bearing on political attitudes. In the early 1980s, Jackson Browne carried the kind of political following that Crosby, Stills, Nash, and Young had in the late 1960s and early 1970s. Yet the fans of Jackson Browne in figure 12.1 cannot be described as liberal. Browne in fact has become a safe, middle-of-the-road draw. The number-one ranked living politician for Browne fans is Gerald Ford; these Browne fans do not relate well to blacks, Jews, or Chicanos. They do relate well to Jesus Christ and the United States, but the fans are repelled by homosexuals, the USSR, and Communists.

Surprisingly, Bruce Springsteen fans appear to be a little more liberal than Jackson Browne fans. Although the Springsteen fans ranked the United States, Jesus Christ, and college students at the top of their list, they ranked Jimmy Carter the highest of living politicians. Moreover, they ranked ERA and women's liberation higher than Browne fans did, and homosexuals higher than Anita Bryant. The Springsteen fans in the survey could hardly be called liberal radicals, but their rankings of the political symbols showed that they are just a little more to the left than the followers of Browne.

Finally, figure 12.3 indicates that punk rock/new wave fans are more liberal than both Springsteen and Browne fans, yet their top rankings of United States, Jesus Christ, Martin Luther King, Jr., and college students shows that they are not a group to be feared by the elite. Punk rock/new wave fans ranked John Anderson as top living politician and they gave Karl Marx a positive ranking. Yet the fans of this style of music ranked Communists near the bottom of their list, along with Arabs, USSR, oil companies, and Anita Bryant.

Fig. 12.1
Jackson Browne fans
political symbols test
Fairfield University, Fall 1980–Spring 1981

Party Identification: 23 Republicans   14 Independent
       7 Independents   Republicans
     24 Democrats   11 Independent
                      Democrats

Ideology: 17 Conservative   39 Middle of the Road
      22 Liberal   1 Radical Leftist

Sex: 45 Female   34 Male

Average Age: 19.9 years

Symbols	Score	Symbols	Score
1. Jackson Browne	158	19. ERA	51
2. Jesus Christ	136	20. John Anderson	45
3. U.S.A.	136	21. Legalized	
4. College students	135	marijuana	45
5. Pope John Paul II	103	22. Jane Fonda	37
6. JFK	102	23. Ronald Reagan	27
7. Catholics	93	24. Protestants	27
8. Whites	91	25. Labor unions	26
9. Baseball	88	26. Ted Kennedy	26
10. Martin Luther		27. U.S. military	14
King, Jr.	85	28. Large corpora-	
11. Lawyers	80	tions	13
12. Supreme Court	73	29. Gloria Steinem	6
13. College professors	68	30. Blacks	3
14. Congress	61	31. Jews	3
15. Democrats	60	32. Socialized medicine	− 3
16. Gerald Ford	58	33. Jimmy Carter	− 6
17. Women's		34. Punk rock/	
liberation	55	new wave	− 7
18. Republicans	51	35. Legalized abortion	− 13

(*Fig. 12.1 continued*)

Symbols	Score	Symbols	Score
36. Karl Marx	− 13	44. Oil companies	− 57
37. CIA	− 14	45. Arabs	− 58
38. Country and western	− 22	46. Nuclear power plants	− 64
39. Chicanos	− 26	47. Draft registration	− 67
40. Atheists	− 28	48. Homosexuals	− 68
41. Richard Nixon	− 36	49. USSR	− 91
42. Busing	− 55	50. Communists	− 95
43. Anita Bryant	− 56		

Fig. 12.2.
Bruce Springsteen fans
political symbols test
Fairfield University, Spring 1980

Party Identification: 12 Republicans 3 Independent
  7 Independents Republicans
  18 Democrats 7 Independent
  Democrats

Ideology: 8 Conservative 23 Middle of the Road 15 Liberal
  1 Radical Leftist

Sex: 22 Female 25 Male

Average Age: 19.6 years

Symbols	Score	Symbols	Score
1. Bruce Spring- steen	90	5. Catholics	62
		6. Lawyers	54
2. U.S.A.	80	7. Martin Luther King, Jr.	52
3. Jesus Christ	77		
4. College students	71	8. JFK	52

(*Fig. 12.2 continued*)

Symbols	Score	Symbols	Score
9. College professors	46	28. George Bush	10
10. Democrats	43	29. Gloria Steinem	7
11. Congress	42	30. Olympic boycott	6
12. ERA	42	31. Jews	2
13. Supreme Court	41	32. Chicanos	2
14. Legalized		33. Ted Kennedy	1
marijuana	37	34. Ronald Reagan	– 3
15. Women's		35. Large corporations	– 4
liberation	34	36. Jesse Jackson	– 7
16. Basketball	31	37. Karl Marx	– 7
17. Affirmative		38. CIA	– 10
action	31	39. Legalized abortion	– 13
18. Republicans	29	40. Jerry Brown	– 14
19. Jimmy Carter	29	41. Busing	– 18
20. Protestants	29	42. Richard Nixon	– 25
21. Socialized		43. Punk rock/new	
medicine	29	wave	– 26
22. Labor unions	27	44. Homosexuals	– 31
23. Increased		45. Nuclear power	
defense		plants	– 35
spending	27	46. Arabs	– 38
24. Blacks	25	47. Anita Bryant	– 38
25. U.S. Army	23	48. USSR	– 57
26. Jane Fonda	16	49. Oil companies	– 59
27. Gerald Ford	14	50. Ayatollah Khomeni	– 85

Fig. 12.3.
Punk Rock/New Wave fans
political symbols test
Fairfield University, Fall 1980 and Spring 1981

Party Identification: 11 Republicans   3 Independent
                          13 Independents   Republicans
(*continued on page 182*)

(Fig. 12.3 continued)

Party Identification: 20 Democrats   13 Independent
                                                          Democrats
                                                     1 Socialist

Ideology: 10 Conservative   23 Middle of the Road   23 Liberal
                  5 Radical Leftist

Sex: 25 Female   36 Male

Average Age: 19.88 years

Symbols	Score	Symbols	Score
1. Punk rock/new wave	122	21. Jane Fonda	25
2. U.S.A.	94	22. Labor Unions	22
3. Jesus Christ	90	23. Jackson Browne	19
4. Martin Luther King, Jr.	74	24. Gerald Ford	17
5. College students	71	25. Blacks	16
6. Legalized marijuana	62	26. Ronald Reagan	15
7. Catholics	58	27. Karl Marx	14
8. Whites	56	28. Socialized medicine	13
9. Pope John Paul II	55	29. Bruce Springsteen	12
10. JFK	54	30. U.S. military	10
11. Lawyers	54	31. Increased defense spending	9
12. College professors	53	32. George Bush	9
13. ERA	52	33. Ted Kennedy	9
14. Supreme Court	52	34. Republicans	7
15. Women's liberation	48	35. Basketball	5
16. Baseball	44	36. Affirmative action	5
17. Democrats	43	37. Legalized abortion	4
18. Protestants	36	38. Jews	2
19. John Anderson	31	39. Jimmy Carter	0
20. Congress	28	40. Chicanos	− 3

(*Fig. 12.3 continued*)

Symbols	Score	Symbols	Score
41. Large corporations	– 4	51. Nuclear power plants	– 29
42. Jesse Jackson	– 7	52. Busing	– 30
43. Olympic boycott	– 7	53. Draft registration	– 32
44. Jerry Brown	– 8	54. Homosexuals	– 34
45. Gloria Steinem	– 9	55. Communists	– 44
46. Atheists	– 10	56. Arabs	– 46
47. Country and western	– 11	57. USSR	– 52
48. CIA	– 13	58. Oil companies	– 52
49. Ayatollah Khomeni	– 18	59. Anita Bryant	– 53
50. Richard Nixon	– 25		

In the late 1960s and early 1970s there was a minimal amount of political predictability from a poll of favorite rock groups. The 1980s offers almost no predictability of political beliefs and attitudes from musical tastes. Most rock music of the 1980s is clearly apolitical, and this seems to be an accurate reflection of the apolitical state of the 1980s rock fan. If, however, the 1980s become more politicized because of economic conditions, the worldwide antinuclear movement, and Third World struggles, then rock music of the 1980s will reflect the dissent and discord among its listeners.

Perhaps the events of September 19, 1981, reflect lack of politicization in rock in the early 1980s. On a day when 100,000 people marched in Washington to protest the Reagan administration's budget cuts, more than 400,000 turned out in Central Park in New York to hear a free Simon and Garfunkel reunion concert. More people turned out to celebrate the myth, the good times, the caring and communal feelings, and the politics of the 1960s in the form of a Paul Simon and Art Garfunkel show than to do the "real thing" in the 1980s, march on Washington for a political cause.

But another model for rock and politics to take in the 1980s was provided by rock superstars and their contribution to nuclear disarmament rallies in 1982. On June 6, 1982, some 90,000 people attended a concert in the Rose Bowl to support a freeze on nuclear weapons. Over $250,000 was raised through concert revenues for the antinuclear weapons movement as concertgoers heard from Bob Dylan, Joan Baez, Stevie Wonder, Linda Ronstadt, David Crosby, Stephen Stills, Graham Nash, Bette Midler, Bonnie Raitt, Dan Fogelberg, Stevie Nicks, Tom Petty, and others.

On June 8, 1982, in Denver, over 30,000 attended a rally and heard from Jimmy Buffett, John Denver, and Judy Collins. In New York on June 9 and 10, 1982, concerts were given by James Taylor, Jackson Browne, and Linda Ronstadt to raise money for the nuclear freeze movement.

To end the week of antinuclear activity on June 12, 800,000 people marched against nuclear weapons in New York to coincide with the opening of the United Nations disarmament conference. This was the largest political demonstration ever held in the United States. Some 600,000 persons tried to jam their way into Central Park to continue the rally. The demonstrators heard political speeches along with songs from Bruce Springsteen, Jackson Browne, Linda Ronstadt, James Taylor, Joan Baez, Rita Marley (Bob Marley's widow), and Gary "U.S." Bonds, among others. This late model of rock and politics made it clear that if movement politics sufficiently politicize an issue at the grass roots level, there would then be no lack of concerned rock stars to provide leadership.

Notes

Chapter 1: Rock and Destruction: Elite Responses to Rock Music

1. Alan Bloom, ed., *The Republic of Plato* (New York: Basic Books, 1968), p. 102.
2. Ibid.
3. Friedrich Nietzsche, *The Birth of Tragedy* (New York: Doubleday Anchor Books, 1956), p. 105.
4. Ibid., p. 124.
5. Steve Chapple and Reebee Garofalo, *Rock'n'Roll Is Here to Pay* (Chicago: Nelson-Hall, 1977), pp. 56-57.
6. Carl Belz, *The Story of Rock* (New York: Oxford Univ. Press, 1972), p. 59.
7. Jerry Hopkins, *The Rock Story* (New York: Signet, 1970), p. 31.
8. Paul Dickson, "Eyes Rock Crammer," *Eye*, May 1968.
9. Hopkins, *Rock Story*, p. 51.
10. Ibid., p. 49.
11. Bob Somma, "Nixonization of Rock," *Fusion*, Dec. 1972.
12. "Agnew vs. the White Rabbit," *Rolling Stone*, oct. 20, 1970, p. 24.
13. Joe Eszterhas, "The Inaugural: Hail to the Chief, Bury the Dead," *Rolling Stone*, Mar. 1, 1973, p. 38.

14. "President Nixon's Fave Raves," *Rolling Stone*, Apr. 16, 1970, p. 9.
15. "Richard Nixon Battles Dopers," *Rolling Stone*, Nov. 26, 1970, p. 6.
16. Ibid.
17. "Worcester Gives Joe a F-U-C-K," *Rolling Stone*, Apr. 16, 1970, p. 17.
18. "Janis Fined $200 for Offending Cops," *Rolling Stone*, Apr. 12, 1970, p. 18.
19. "Rock and Roll's Real Dirty," *Rolling Stone*, Apr. 2, 1970, p. 12.
20. Ibid.
21. Ben Fong-Torres, "Jim Morrison's Got the Blues," *Rolling Stone*, Mar. 4, 1971, p. 22.
22. Marshall Rosenthal "Chicago: The First Interracial Riot," *Rolling Stone*, Sept. 3, 1970, p. 14.
23. *New York Times*, Sept. 12, 1972, p. 19.
24. Ben Fong-Torres, "Drugola Inquiry: Senator Claims Columbia Gag," *Rolling Stone*, Aug. 16, 1973, p. 8.
25. James Buckley, Senator, *Congressional Record*, Senate, Nov. 21, 1973, vol. 119, no. 180, reprint.
26. Ibid.
27. Ibid.
28. Ibid.
29. "Bulletin on Narcotics," Department of Economic and Social Affairs, United Nations, Oct./Dec. 1969.
30. Ibid.
31. Buckley (see note 25).
32. Ibid.
33. Ibid.
34. Ibid.
35. *Rolling Stone*, Aug. 1, 1974, p. 9.
36. Hunter S. Thompson, *Fear and Loathing on the Campaign Trail '72* (New York: Popular Library, 1973).
37. Frederick Dutton, *Changing Sources of Power: American Politics in the 1970s* (New York: McGraw-Hill, 1971), p. 16.
38. Ibid., p. 19.
39. Ben Fong-Torres, "Stars Come Out for McGovern," *Rolling Stone*, May 11, 1972, p. 8.
40. Robin Green, "McGovern? He's a Baaaad Mother," *Rolling Stone*, June 8, 1972, p. 18.
41. Ibid.
42. "New York Rallies: Newman Bugs Out," *Rolling Stone*, July 20, 1972, p. 20.

43. John Gibson, "MGM Pushes for Richard Nixon," *Rolling Stone,* Nov. 9, 1972, p. 16.

44. Ibid.

45. Joe Klein and Dave Marsh, "Rock and Politics," *Rolling Stone,* Sept. 9, 1976, pp. 30-35.

46. Maureen Orth, "Battle of the Bands," *Newsweek,* May 31, 1976, p. 44.

Chapter 2: Student Activism, Rock Music, and Social Change

1. Philip Altbach, *Student Politics in America: A Historical Analysis* (New York: McGraw-Hill, 1974). Altbach notes historical perspectives in student activism in the 1930s and 1960s.

2. James Wood, *The Sources of Student Activism* (Lexington, Mass: D. C. Heath, 1974). Wood dates student activism to the 1964 Berkeley free speech movement.

3. The May Day activities of 1971 mark the end of large-scale student activism.

4. Richard Peterson, *The Scope of Organized Student Protest 1967-1968* (Princeton, N.J.: Educational Testing Service, 1968); Richard Peterson and John Bilorusky, *May 1970: The Campus Aftermath of Cambodia and Kent State* (Washington: Carnegie Commission on Higher Education, 1971); *The Report of President's Commission on Campus Unrest* (New York: Arno Press, 1970); and Garth Buchanan and Joan Brackett, *Survey of Campus Incidents as Interpreted by College Presidents, Faculty Chairmen, and Student Body Presidents* (Washington, D.C.: Urban Institute, 1971).

5. Peterson and Bilorusky, *May 1970.* Gives statistics for participation in campus protest activity for May 1970.

6. Paul Walton, "The Case of the Weathermen," in *Politics and Deviance,* I. Taylor and L. Taylor, eds. (New York, Penguin Books, 1973), p. 157.

7. John Mueller, *War, Presidents and Public Opinion* (New York: Wiley, 1973).

8. See Robert Dahl, *After the Revolution* (Yale Univ. Press, 1970).

9. Brian Salter, "Explanations of Student Unrest: An Exercise in Devaluation," *British Journal of Sociology,* Sept. 1973, p. 334.

10. Ibid., pp. 335-36.

11. Jack Dennis, ed., *Socialization to Politics: A Reader* (New York: Wiley, 1973). Contains much of Easton and Dennis socialization work.

12. Fred Greenstein, *Children and Politics,* rev. ed. (New Haven, Conn.: Yale Univ. Press, 1969).

13. Robert Hess and Judith Torney, *The Development of Political Attitudes in Children* (Garden City, N.Y.: Anchor Books, 1968).
14. What is a system-maintaining attitude? In Easton's and Dennis's terms, it is one that shows support for the system. But this overlooks the demand function. Citizens must make demands upon the political system or the system will collapse.
15. Salter, "Explanations of Student Unrest," p. 334.
16. Theodore Roszak, "Youth and the Great Refusal," in *The Politics and the Anti-Politics of the Young*, Michael Brown, ed. (Beverly Hills, Cal.: Glencoe Press, 1969), pp. 3-21. See also Charles Reich, *The Greening of America* (New York: Bantam Books, 1971).
17. Peterson and Bilorusky, *May 1970*, introduction. Even during May 1970, not all young people participated in protest activities.
18. Ibid. Bilorusky focuses on Berkeley radicals; James Wood has written an excellent book, *Sources of Student Activism*, on Berkeley radicals, which suffers from methodological problems. Wood generalizes from the Berkeley sample to explain student dissent all over the country.
19. See Kenneth Keniston, "Becoming a Radical," in *Political Socialization*, Edward Greenberg, ed. (New York: Atherton, 1970), pp. 110-50.
20. Hess and Torney, *Development of Political Attitudes*, pp. 24-25.
21. See Sigmund Freud, *Totem and Taboo* (New York: Norton, 1950), and Freud's *Group Psychology and the Analysis of the Ego* (New York: Bantam, 1960).
22. Lewis Feuer, *The Conflict of Generations* (New York: Basic Books, 1969).
23. Ibid.
24. Ibid., chapter 10.
25. Kenneth Keniston, *Young Radicals: Notes on Committed Youth* (New York: Harcourt, Brace and World, 1968), pp. 46-48.
26. Joel Aberbach, "Alienation and Political Behavior," in S. Kirkpatrick and L. Pettit, eds. *The Social Psychology of Political Life* (Belmont, Cal.: Duxbury Press, 1972), pp. 58-71.
27. Kenneth Keniston, *The Uncommitted: Alienated Youth in American Society* (New York: Harcourt, Brace, and World, 1965), p. 454.
28. Keniston, "Becoming a Radical," p. 148.
29. Robert Lane, "Meeting Needs in Political Life," in *The Social Psychology of Political Life*, S. Kirkpatrick and L. Pettit, eds. (Belmont, Cal.: Duxbury Press, 1972), p. 180.
30. Ibid. p. 281.

31. Lester Milbrath, *Political Participation*. (Chicago: Rand McNally, 1965), p. 29.

32. Ibid.

33. Ibid., p. 12.

34. Richard Merelman, "The Development of Policy Thinking in Adolescence," *APSR*, Dec. 1971, pp. 1033-47.

35. Norma Haan, Brewster Smith, and Jeanne Block, "Moral Reasoning of Young Adults: Political-Social Behavior, Family Backgrounds and Personality Correlates," *Journal of Personality and Social Psychology*, Nov. 1968, pp. 183-201.

36. Ibid., p. 183.

37. Lawrence Kohlberg, "Moral and Religious Education and the Public Schools: A Developmental View," in *Religion and Public Education*, T. R. Sizer, ed. (New York: Houghton Mifflin, 1967).

38. Haan, Smith, and Block, "Moral Reasoning," p. 199.

39. Ibid., p. 195.

40. Richard Flacks, "The Liberated Generation: An Exploration of the Roots of Student Protest," *Journal of Social Issues*, July 1967, pp. 66-67.

41. Keniston, *Young Radicals*, p. 46.

42. Seymour Lipset, *Rebellion in the University* (Boston: Little, Brown, 1972), p. 80.

43. Stephen Douglas, *Political Socialization and Student Activism in Indonesia* (Champaign: Univ. of Illinois Press, 1970), p. 26.

44. Ellis Krauss, *Japanese Radicals Revisited* (Berkeley: Univ. of California Press, 1974), p. 52.

45. Wood, *Sources*, p. xvi.

46. Phillip Altback, "Students and Politics," in *Student Politics*, Seymour Lipset, ed. (New York: Basic Books, 1967), p. 52.

47. Ibid., p. 78.

48. Ibid., p. viii.

49. Ibid.

50. Kenneth Kolson, "The Politics of Expression: Political Socialization and Campus Activism," paper delivered at the annual meeting of the Midwest Political Science Assn., Chicago, May 1973, p. 52.

51. Ibid., p. 49.

52. Jeffery Page, "Political Orientation and Riot Participation," *American Sociological Review*, Oct. 1971, p. 810.

53. Ken Langton and M. Kent Jennings, "Political Socialization and the High School Civics Curriculum in the United States," *APSR*, Sept. 1968, pp. 852-68.

54. Richard Merelman, *Political Socialization and Educational Climates* (New York: Holt, Rinehart and Winston, 1971), chapters 3 and 4.
55. John Grove, Richard Remy, and Harmon Zeigler, "Political Socialization and Political Ideology as Sources of Educational Discontent," *Social Sciences Quarterly,* Sept. 1974, pp. 411-24.
56. Ibid., p. 414.
57. James Simon Kunen, *The Strawberry Statement: Notes of a College Revolutionary* (New York: Avon, 1970).
58. Michael Brown, "Alienation among Middle Class Young: Politics, Drugs and Ambisexualism," paper delivered at the annual meeting of the Midwest Political Science Assn., Chicago, May 1973.
59. Reich, *Greening of America,* introduction.
60. Ibid., pp. 262-69.
61. Philip Nobile, ed., *Con III Controversy: The Critics Look at the Greening of America,* (New York: Pocket Books, 1971), p. 31.
62. Ralph Gleason, "Perspective," in *Age of Paranoia,* (New York: Pocket Book, 1972), p. 404.
63. Nobile, *Con III Controversy,* p. 13.
64. Ibid.
65. Ibid.
66. Ellen Willis quoted in Nobile, *Con III Controversy,* p. 227.
67. Nobile, *Con III Controversy,* p. 232.
68. R. Serge Denisoff, *Sing a Song of Social Significance* (Bowling Green, Ohio: Bowling Green State Univ. Popular Press, 1972), p. ix.
69. Ibid., p. x.
70. Ibid.
71. Brown, "Alienation," p. 9.
72. Ibid.
73. Ibid., p. 10.
74. Ibid.
75. Ibid., p. 13.
76. Ibid., p. 18.
77. Ibid., p. 19.
78. William S. Fox and James D. Williams, "Political Orientation and Music Preferences among College Students," *Public Opinion Quarterly,* Fall 1974, pp. 352-71.
79. Ibid., p. 371.
80. Paul Abramson, "Political Efficacy and Political Trust among Black Schoolchildren: Two Explanations," *Journal of Politics,* June 1972, pp. 1243-69.

81. Donald Thistlethwaite, "Impact of Disruptive External Events on Student Attitudes," *Journal of Personality and Social Psychology*, Spring 1974, pp. 228-42.
82. Richard Merelman, "The Development of Policy Thinking in Adolescence," *APSR*, Dec. 1971, p. 1047.
83. Altbach, *Student Politics in America*. See also Charles Chatfield, "Pacifists and Their Publics: The Politics of the Peace Movement," *Midwest Journal of Politics*, May 1968; and Michael Lipsky, "Protest as a Political Resource," *APSR*, Dec. 1968.
84. Anthony Downs, *An Economic Theory of Democracy* (New York: Harper and Row), 1957.
85. James Buchanan and Gordon Tullock, *The Calculus of Consent* (Ann Arbor: Univ. of Michigan Press, 1965). Offers a political economist's view of particular political phenomena.

Chapter 3: The Marijuana Policies of the United States

1. Lester Grinspoon, *Marijuana Reconsidered* (New York: Bantam Books, 1971), p. 12.
2. Ibid., p. 14.
3. Ibid.
4. "War and the Dope Habit," *Literary Digest*, June 9, 1917, p. 1777.
5. Ibid.
6. "The Superstitions of Dope," *Literary Digest*, June 30, 1919, p. 1990.
7. Arnold H. Taylor, *American Diplomacy and the Narcotics Traffic 1900-1939* (Durham, N.C.: Duke Univ. Press, 1969), p. 129.
8. Ibid., p. 132.
9. Joseph P. Chamberlain, "Dope Situation as Congress Faces It," *Survey*, Sept. 6, 1919, p. 798.
10. David E. Smith, *The New Social Drug* (Englewood Cliffs, N.J.: Prentice-Hall, 1970), p. 107.
11. "Indian Hemp Commission Report—1894," *Transaction*, Dec. 1969, p. 10.
12. Grinspoon, *Marijuana Reconsidered*, p. 22.
13. Robert P. Walton, *Marijuana* (New York: Lippincott, 1938), p. 39.
14. Grinspoon, Marijuana Reconsidered, p. 18.
15. "Marijuana Menaces Youth," *Scientific American*, Mar. 1936, p. 150.
16. Taylor, *American Diplomacy*, p. 291.
17. "Facts and Fancies about Marijuana," *Literary Digest* Oct. 24, 1936, pp. 7-8.

18. H. J. Anslinger, *The Murderers* (New York: Farrar, Straus, Cuday, 1961), p. 38.
19. Smith, *New Social Drug*, p. 110.
20. Joel Fort, "Drug Use and the Law," *Current*, Dec. 1969, p. 7.
21. Smith, *New Social Drug*, p. 111.
22. "Marijuana Law, "*New Republic*, Mar. 23, 1968, p. 9-10.
23. H. J. Anslinger, "Marijuana—Assassin of Youth," *Reader's Digest*, Feb. 1938, p. 3.
24. Ibid., p. 6.
25. "Marijuana—More Dangerous Than Heroin or Cocaine," *Scientific American*, May 1938, p. 293.
26. "Marijuana Seen as Epidemic among Idle," *Science News Letter*, Nov. 1938, p. 340.
27. Grinspoon, *Marijuana Reconsidered*, p. 30.
28. "Review of Mayor's Committee," *Science*, May 25, 1945, p. 539.
29. "The Menace of Marijuana," *Science Digest*, July 1945, p. 50.
30. Anslinger, *Murderers*, p. 41.
31. "Army Study of Marijuana Smokers," *Newsweek*, Jan. 15, 1945, p. 72.
32. Earl Wilson, "Crazy Dreamers," *Collier's*, June 4, 1949, p. 27.
33. Ibid.
34. "The Wicked Weed," *Science Digest*, Apr. 1952, p. 48.
35. Grinspoon, *Marijuana Reconsidered*, p. 379.
36. Ibid., p. 380.
37. Charles A. Reich, *The Greening of America* (New York: Bantam Books, 1970), p. 281.
38. Ibid.
39. Ibid., p. 353.
40. "Crackdown," *Nation*, Mar. 10, 1969, p. 293.
41. Smith, *New Social Drug*, p. 183.
42. Ibid., p. 113.
43. Ibid., p. 114.
44. Fort, "Drug Use," p. 13.
45. "Pot Penalties Too Severe," *Science News*, Oct. 8, 1966, p. 270.
46. Ibid.
47. A. T. Weil, "On Effects of Marijuana," *Science*, Mar. 14, 1969, p. 1145.
48. "Nixon's New Plan," *U.S. News and World Report*, Oct. 8, 1969, p. 14.
49. Ibid.
50. Ibid.

51. Kenneth Crawford, "Vogues in Vice," *Newsweek*, Nov. 10, 1969, p. 45.
52. John Keats, "Appraising Marijuana—The National Pastime," *Holiday*, Apr. 1970, p. 53.

Chapter 4: Rock Music and Political Attitudes

1. Fred I. Greenstein, "Political Socialization," *International Encyclopedia of the Social Sciences*, vol. 14 (New York: Crowell-Collier and Macmillan, 1968), p. 551.
2. Gabriel Almond, "A Functional Approach to Comparative Politics," in *The Politics of Developing Areas*, G. Almond and J. Coleman, eds. (Princeton, N.J.: Princeton Univ. Press, 1960), p. 28.
3. Margaret Conway and Frank Feigart, *Political Analysis: An Introduction* (Boston: Allyn and Bacon, 1972).
4. V. O. Key has suggested that about one of every four Americans is an opinion leader.
5. William McGuire, "The Nature of Attitudes and Attitude Change," in *Handbook of Social Psychology*, vol. 3, G. Lindzey and E. Aronson, eds. (Reading, Mass.: Addison-Wesley, 1968), p. 174.
6. Robert Levine, "The Role of the Family in Authority Systems: A Cross Cultural Application of Stimulus Generalization Theory," *Behavioral Science*, Oct. 1960, p. 295.
7. Paul Hirsch, "Sociological Approaches to Pop Music," *American Behavioral Scientist*, Jan. 1971, p. 372.
8. T. Horton, "The Dialogue of Courtship in Popular Songs," *American Journal of Sociology*, May 1957, p. 569-78.
9. James Carey, "Changing Courtship Patterns in Popular Song," *American Journal of Sociology*, May 1969, p. 730.
10. Hirsch, "Sociological Approaches," p. 374.
11. Carey, "Changing Courtship Patterns," p. 731.
12. P. F. Sloan, "Eve of Destruction," ABC/Dunhill, 1965.
13. R. S. Denisoff, *Sing a Song of Social Significance* (Bowling Green, Ohio: Bowling Green State Univ. Popular Press, 1972), p. 139.
14. Ibid., pp. 139-40.
15. Ibid., pp. 150-51.
16. Hirsch, "Sociological Approaches," p. 376.
17. Ibid., p. 377.
18. Ibid., p. 378.
19. Ibid., p. 380.

20. Steven Levine, *Political Socialization, Student Radicalism and American Political Science,* Ph.D. dissertation, Florida State Univ., 1971 (Ann Arbor, Mich., University Microfilms, 1971).
21. Karl Schuessler, "Social Background and Musical Taste," American Sociological Review, June 1948, p. 333.
22. Ibid., p. 335.
23. David Voelker, "You Tell Me Your Three Favorite Rock Groups, and I'll Tell You Whether or Not You Believe in God or Anything Else," *Circular,* Feb. 4, 1974, p. 1.
24. Ibid.
25. Ibid., p. 4.
26. Ibid.
27. Dr. John Mood, in his lectures on the "Poetry of Rock Music" at Ball State University, Muncie, Ind., 1972.
28. Perhaps this finding is not so remarkable after all. Alice Cooper was all-American, violent, fascist on stage, and he drank only beer. He was a golf fanatic and a country clubber. He was a millionaire, and he supported Richard Nixon in 1972.

Chapter 5: Bob Dylan

1. "Bob Dylan Interview," *Saturday Evening Post,* July 30, 1966, p. 65.
2. Bob Dylan, liner notes from *"Bringin' It All Back Home,"* by Bob Dylan, Columbia Records, 1965.
3. "Bringin' It All Back Home," by Bob Dylan.
4. D. A. Pennebacker, *Don't Look Back* (New York: Ballantine, 1968), p. 128.
5. *Saturday Evening Post,* July 3, 1966, p. 68.
6. Pennebaker, *Don't Look Back,* p. 43.
7. Jon Landau, "John Wesley Harding," in *Age of Rock,* Jon Eisen, ed. (New York: Vintage Books, 1969), p. 219.
8. Anthony Scaduto, *Bob Dylan: An Intimate Biography,* as quoted in *Rolling Stone,* March 2, 1972, p. 41.
9. Ibid.
10. Ibid., March 16, 1972, p. 46.
11. Ibid.
12. "Playboy Interview," in *Dylan: A Commemoration,* Stephen Pickering, ed. (Berkeley, Calif.: Book People, 1971), p. 31.
13. Paul Robbins, "Bob Dylan as Bob Dylan," in Pickering, *Dylan,* p. 17.
14. Theodore Roszak, quoted in Pickering, *Dylan,* p. 40.
15. Scott Sullivan, "Bob Dylan's Dreams," in Pickering, *Dylan,* p. 40.

16. Bob Dylan, "George Jackson," Columbia Records, 1971.
17. "Ole Bob Dylan: Everybody Wants Me to Be Just Like Them," *Rolling Stone*, Jan. 1972, p. 10.
18. Anthony Scaduto, "Won't You Listen to the Lambs, Bob Dylan?" in *Rolling Stone*, Jan. 6, 1972, p. 10.
19. Ibid.

Chapter 6: The Rolling Stones

1. Bobby Abrams, "What Motherfuckin' Heavies," in *The Age of Rock 2*, Jonathan Eisen, ed. (New York: First Vintage Books, 1970), p. 44.
2. Mick Jagger and Keith Richards, "Satisfaction," London Records, 1965.
3. Robert Somma, "Rock Theatricality," *Drama Review*, Fall 1969, p. 132.
4. Ibid., p. 133.
5. Lester Bangs, in *The Rolling Stone Record Review* (New York: Straight Arrow Pub., Pocket Book, 1971), p. 108.
6. Abrams, "What Motherfuckin' Heavies," p. 48.
7. Michael Lydon, "The Rolling Stones at Play in the Apocalypse," *Ramparts*, Jan. 1970, p. 42.
8. Jay Marks, "Women in Rock," *Vogue*, Mar. 1971, p. 112.
9. Ibid.
10. Richard Merton, "Comment," in *The Age of Rock*, Jonathan Eisen, ed. (New York, N.Y.: First Vintage Books, 1969), p. 116.
11. Ibid.
12. Tom Nolan, "Groupies: A Story of Our Time," in Eisen, *Age of Rock*, pp. 77-93.
13. Abrams, "What Motherfuckin' Heavies," p. 49.
14. Mick Jagger and Keith Richards, "Back Street Girl," London Records, 1967.
15. Marks, "Women in Rock," p. 113.
16. Ellen Willis, "The Women's Movement in Rock," *New Yorker*, Oct. 23, 1971, p. 169.
17. Mick Jagger and Keith Richards, "Midnight Rambler," London Records, 1969.
18. Geoffrey Cannon, "Age of Aquarius," *Partisan Review*, Spring 1969, p. 25.
19. Frank McConnell, "Rock and the Politics of Frivolity," *Massachusetts Review*, Winter 1971, p. 134.
20. "Rose Petals and Revolution," *Time*, Nov. 28, 1969, p. 90.
21. Cannon, "Age of Aquarius," p. 286.

22. I was in the balcony overhanging the stage at the Stones' concert, Chicago International Amphitheater, 1969.
23. McConnell, "Rock," p. 131.
24. Cannon, "Age of Aquarius," p. 286.
25. Jon Landau, in *Rolling Stone Record Review* (New York: Straight Arrow Pub., Pocket Books, 1971), p. 101.
26. Ibid., p. 100.
27. Lydon, "Rolling Stones at Play," p. 42.
28. Richard Neville, "Paint It Black, You Devil," *Creem*, Oct. 1971, pp. 27-30.

Chapter 7: John Lennon

1. John Lennon and Paul McCartney, "Revolution," from *White*, Capital Records, 1968.
2. "Working Class Hero," from *John Lennon Plastic Ono Band*, Apple Records, 1970.
3. John Lennon, "God," from *Plastic Ono Band*, Apple Records, 1970.
4. John Lennon, "Imagine."
5. Stu Worbin, "John and Jerry and David and John and Leni and Yoko," *Rolling Stone*, Feb. 17, 1972, p. 12.
6. Ibid., p. 8.
7. "Lennon: Back in the U.S.S.A.," *Rolling Stone*, Oct. 10, 1974, p. 11.
8. Ralph Gleason, "Perspectives: Fair Play for John and Yoko," *Rolling Stone*, June 22, 1972, p. 34.
9. John Lennon and Yoko Ono, record sleeve of *Mind Games*, Apple Records, 1973.

Chapter 9: Rock Politicos

1. Richard Goldstein, *The Poetry of Rock Music* (New York: Bantam Books, 1968), p. 100.
2. Stephen Stills, "For What It's Worth," ATCO Cotillion Music and Ten East Music, 1966.
3. Stephen Stills, "Find the Cost of Freedom," Goldhill Music, 1970, from *4 Way Street*, by Crosby, Stills, Nash, and Young, Atlantic Records, 1970.
4. Graham Nash, "Chicago," Giving Room Music, 1970, from *4 Way Street*, by Crosby, Stills, Nash and Young, Atlantic Records, 1970.
5. David Crosby, "Long Time Gone," Guerrilla Music, 1968.
6. Neil Young, "Ohio," Broken Arrow/Cotillion, 1970.
7. Neil Young, "Southern Men," Broken Arrow/Cotillion, 1970.
8. Van Zant, "Sweet Home Alabama," Rossington and King, Duchess Music Corp./Hustlers Inc., 1974.

9. Neil Young, "After the Gold Rush," Broken Arrow/Cotillion, 1970.

10. Roger McGuinn and Gram Parsons, "Drug Store Truck Drivin' Man," from *The Best of the Byrds*, vol. 2, 1972.

11. Roger McGuinn and Jacques Levy, "I Wanna Grow Up to Be a Politician," from *The Best of the Byrds*, vol. 2, 1972.

12. Skip Battin and Kim Fowley, "America's Great National Pastime," from *The Best of the Byrds*, vol. 2, 1972.

Chapter 11: The Politics of Rock Music

1. David DeVoss, "Don't Lay No Boogie Woogie on the King of Rock and Roll," *Sound*, 1974-1975, p. 5.

2. Jim Morrison, quoted in *The Movement toward a New America: The Beginnings of a Long Revolution* (New York: Random House, 1970), p. 394.

3. Country Joe McDonald, in *The Rolling Stone Interviews*, vol. 2 (New York: Warner, 1973), p. 185.

4. Ben Fong-Torres, "Shattered Dreams in Motor City," *Rolling Stone*, June 8, 1971, pp. 30-31.

5. Judith Sims, "Chicago: A James William Guercio Enterprise," *Rolling Stone*, July 19, 1973, p. 23.

6. Jon Landau, "Rock 1970: It's Too Late to Stop Now," *Rolling Stone*, Dec. 2, 1970, p. 41.

7. LeRoi Jones, "The Changing Scene," in *Black Music* (New York: Morrow, 1968), p. 205.

8. Gallup Youth Survey, *Indianapolis Star*, June 22, 1977, p. 32.

9. Ibid.

10. Ibid.

11. Robert W. Turner, *I'll Never Lie to You* (New York: Ballantine, 1976), p. 95.

12. Ibid., p. 96.

13. Chet Flippo, "Phil Ochs, Troubadour, Dead: He was a Child of the 60s," *Rolling Stone*, May 20, 1976, p. 12.

14. Dave Marsh, "Singing for the World's Supper," *Rolling Stone*, Apr. 6, 1978, p. 32.

15. Ibid., p. 37.

16. Daisann McLane, "MUSE: Rock Politics Comes of Age," *Rolling Stone*, Nov. 15, 1979, p. 10. See also John Rockwell, "Rock Stars Are Into Politics Again," *New York Times*, Sept. 16, 1979, Arts and Leisure section, p. 22; Debra Rae Cohen, "John Hall: Power Is the Only Issue," *Rolling Stone*, Aug. 23, 1979, pp. 18-19.

17. "The Clash: Rebel Rockers Storm the Barricades," *High Times*, Aug. 1979, p. 36.

18. James Henke, "There'll Be Dancing in the Street: The Clash," *Rolling Stone,* Apr. 17, 1980, p. 41.
19. "The Clash," p. 38.
20. Ibid., p. 39.
21. G. B. Trudeau, "The Rolling Stone Interview: Jimmy Thudpucker," *Rolling Stone,* Feb. 9, 1978, pp. 40-43.

Chapter 12: Conclusion

1. Robert Avery, Adolescent Use of Mass Media, in "Use of Mass Media," *American Behavioral Scientist,* Sept./Oct. 1979, p. 63.
2. J. Lyle and H. R. Hoffman, "Children's Use of Television and Other Media," in *Television and Social Behavior,* vol. 4, E. Rubinstein et al., ed. (Washington, D.C.: U.S. Government Printing Office, 1972).
3. Bob Dylan, *Bob Dylan in His Own Words,* Pearce Marchbank, ed. (New York: Quick Fox, 1978), p. 117.
4. Steve Chapple and Reebee Garofalo, *Rock'n'Roll Is Here to Pay* (Chicago: Nelson-Hall, 1977).
5. See Jerome Rodnitzky, *Minstrels of the Dawn: The Folk-Protest Singer as a Cultural Hero* (Chicago: Nelson-Hall, 1976).

Bibliography

Baraka, Imamu Amiri. *Black Music.* New York: Morrow, 1967.

Chapple, Steve, and Garofalo, Reebee. *Rock 'N' Roll Is Here to Pay.* Chicago: Nelson-Hall, 1976.

Davis, Clive, and Willworth, James. *Clive: Inside the Record Business.* New York: Morrow, 1975.

Eisen, Jonathan, ed. *The Age of Rock.* New York: Random House, 1969.

Eisen, Jonathan, ed. *The Age of Rock,* vol. 2. New York: Random House, 1970.

Fong-Torres, Ben, ed. *The Rolling Stone Rock and Roll Reader.* New York: Bantam Books, 1974.

Frith, Simon. *Sound Effects.* New York: Pantheon, 1981.

Lasch, Christopher. *The Culture of Narcissism.* New York: Norton, 1978.

Macken, Bob; Fornatale, Peter; and Ayres, Bill. *The Rock Music Sourcebook.* Garden City, N.Y.: Doubleday, 1980.

Marchbank, Pearce, ed. *Bob Dylan in His Own Words.* New York: Quick Fox, 1978.

Marcus, Greil. *Mystery Train: Images of America in Rock 'n' Roll Music.* New York: Dutton, 1976.

Marsh, Dave, and Stein, Kevin. *The Book of Rock Lists.* New York: Dell, 1981.

Marsh, Dave, and Swenson, John, eds. *The Rolling Stone Record Guide.* New York: Random House/Rolling Stone, 1979.

Miller, Jim, ed. *The Rolling Stone Illustrated History of Rock and Roll,* New York: Random House/Rolling Stone, 1976, 1980.

Nimmo, Dan, and Combs, James. *Subliminal Politics.* Englewood Cliffs, N.J.: Prentice-Hall, 1980.

Nugent, Stephen, and Gillet, Charlie. *Rock Almanac.* Garden City, N.Y.: Doubleday, 1978.

Rodnitzky, Jerome L. *Minstrels of the Dawn: The Folk-Protest Singer as a Cultural Hero.* Chicago: Nelson-Hall, 1976.

Rolling Stone Editors. *Knockin' on Dylan's Door.* New York: Pocket Books, 1974.

Rolling Stone Editors. *The Rolling Stone Interviews.* New York: Paperback Library, 1971.

Rolling Stone Editors. *The Rolling Stone Interviews, vol. 2.* New York: Warner, 1973.

Sheff, David, and Golson, G. Barry, eds. *The Playboy Interviews with John Lennon and Yoko Ono.* New York: Playboy Press, 1981.

Wenner, Jann, ed. *Rolling Stone* magazine, 1969 to 1983.

Index

LIBRARY
ST. LOUIS COMMUNITY COLLEGE
AT FLORISSANT VALLEY